P9-DEA-121

James H. Evans Jr.

WE SHALL ALL BE CHANGED

SOCIAL PROBLEMS AND THEOLOGICAL RENEWAL

Fortress Press
Minneapolis

To Men of the Spirit—

My Uncles,
Walter Oliver, Joe Watson, Charles Hutcheson, and Jesse Burke

In Memoriam,
James Oliver, Theodore Evans, Marshall Evans

My Brothers,
Thomas Eugene and Randolph Leon

My Sons,
James III and Jumaane Haji

I declare to you, brothers and sisters,
that flesh and blood cannot inherit the kingdom of God,
nor does the perishable inherit the imperishable.
Listen, I tell you a mystery:
We will not all sleep, but we shall all be changed.
—1 Corinthians 15:50-52

WE SHALL ALL BE CHANGED
Social Problems and Theological Renewal

Cover and interior design: David Lott
Cover art: Jacob Lawrence, "Builders, Red and Green Ball." Courtesy of the artist and Francine Seders Gallery, Seattle, Washington.

ISBN 0-8006-3084-X

The paper used in this book meets the minimum requirements of American National Standard for Information Sciences—Permanence of Paper for Printed Library Materials, ANSI Z329.48-1984.

Manufactured in the United States of America   AF 1-3084

01   99   98   97   96   1   2   3   4   5   6   7   8   9   10

Contents

Preface

Christians live in the real world, and Christian witness takes place in the context of those problems—both public and personal—that shape human existence. This is especially true for African American Christians. Yet the relations between Christian witness and social problems are complex and require sustained analysis. This book will address three significant social problems within the African American community by offering a theological description of these problems and relating them to specific Christian doctrines. The aim of the book is to assess the ways in which these doctrines both contribute to and ameliorate those problems, and to suggest ways that these problems challenge the Christian community to reconstruct its understanding of these doctrines.

In essence, my hypothesis is that a practical theology for our times cannot be simply the application of preconceived theological understandings to human problems. It must engage those problems initially on their own terms. This theology must critically examine the complicity of Christian thought and the churches in the exacerbation of and relief from those problems. It must contribute to the renewal of Christian teaching and belief with fresh readings of the traditional sources of revelation and insight, in light of those problems.

This book will focus on the relation between social problems and the Christian faith in relation to the African American community. My personal involvement with this particular community is one of the reasons that this perspective has been chosen. But there are other reasons that this particular approach promises to be fruitful. First, the African American community is one of the U.S. populations most visibly affected by what sociologists describe as *social problems*. Second, over time and space, African American churches have consistently been compelled to relate their understanding of Christianity to these problems. Third, the African American Christian tradition has been, at various points in history, exemplary in its ability to balance contemporary concerns with historical commitments. What this project will contribute is a sustained discussion of how engagement with such social concerns alters, reshapes, and renews theological understandings.

This analysis will also have significance for Christian communities in general. Because social problems are the results of conflicting views, visions, and commitments between groups and individuals, there are no problems in the African American community that do not involve society as a whole. Since social problems involve basic issues in human life, there are no social problems that do not have the capacity to challenge our fundamental theological convictions. It is the aim of this book to enhance the possibility of theological engagement with critical issues of the day without falling into either secular nihilism or ecclesiastical triumphalism.

I wish to thank J. Michael West of Fortress Press for his support and assistance and Ms. Stephanie Clark, my administrative assistant, for her help in preparing this manuscript. I also want to express my gratitude to the faculty and administration of Princeton Theological Seminary for the invitation to deliver the 1996 Stone Lectures. Early versions of chapters 2 and 3 were originally presented in that setting. I also want to acknowledge the contribution of my colleagues in the Workgroup on Constructive Theology. An early version of chapter 4 was published as part of the work of that group of scholars. I must give thanks to Dr. Clarice J. Martin for her critical reading of portions of the manuscript and for her steadfast friendship. And I thank my children, James III, Jamila Halima, and Jumaane Haji, for the ongoing honor of being their father.

February 1997
Treasure Cay, Abaco, Bahamas

Social Problems as Theological Problems

Audiences who are estranged from the Church and who would listen to theological terminology with frank scorn, will listen with absorbed interest to religious thought when it is linked with their own social problems.
—Walter Rauschenbusch
A Theology for the Social Gospel

Social problems are not often viewed as the proper subject matter of theology. When they find their way into theological discourse it is usually under the aegis of ethics. But assigning discussion of social problems in theological discourse solely to the field of ethics does justice to neither the field of ethics nor the influence of these problems on Christian witness in our times. Elsewhere I have argued that theology, broadly conceived, and African American theology specifically, is the result of pursuing three distinct but interrelated tasks.[1] The first task involves what is normally called fundamental or foundational theology. The second task involves what is normally called systematic or dogmatic theology. It is the third task, especially as it emerges in African American Christian thought, which concerns us here.

The Tasks of Practical Theology

The third task of African American theology is related to what is called in North American and European theology *practi-*

cal or applied theology. This type of theology has traditionally taken two distinct forms. The first deals with the expression of faith in human society. John Macquarrie describes "applied theology" as that task which is "concerned with the expression of faith in concrete existence, in the institutional, cultic, and ethical aspects of the life of faith."[2] David Tracy describes practical theology as that discipline which is directed toward the techno-economic structures within society and is concerned with the allocation of goods and services, the meaning of social justice, and the realm of culture.[3] Both Macquarrie and Tracy describe this form of theology as one that is turned toward society and concerned with the structures of that society. The second form of this task of theology deals with church organization and the structure of the Christian community. Friedrich Schleiermacher long ago described practical theology as that task which is concerned with church government and church service. It is directed toward the organization of the Christian community.[4] Gerhard Ebeling describes practical theology, rather too neatly, as that task which "presents the special theory of the form of church leadership, while the other disciplines develop the theory of what constitutes the content of the practice of church leadership."[5] Both Schleiermacher and Ebeling relate practical theology to the ecclesiastical life of the community.

Practical theology as described by Macquarrie and Tracy shares an affinity with traditional political theology. Hugo Assmann states that such a theology normally "starts as a 'theological' justification for 'reasons of state'; the clear ideological aim is to legitimize the status quo."[6] The affinity is a shared concern for the societal-institutional manifestations of the life of faith. Practical theology as described by Schleiermacher and Ebeling is concerned with the ecclesiastical-institutional manifestations of the life of faith. The major deficiency in both these ways of defining practical theology is that both are institutionally bound. For Tracy and Macquarrie, the idea of "the state" as a justly ordered polis dominates practical theology. For Schleiermacher and Ebeling, the idea of "the church" as divinely ordered political community dominates practical theology. For African American theologians the notions of both the "state" and the "church" are problematic and open to question. In a land where African Americans have been oppressed by the despotic notions of the state and excluded by truncated notions of the church, theocracy or a narrow ecclesiasticism become suspect as points of departure for practical theology. Moreover, when notions of the state and the church are collapsed, obscuring the distinctive role of each in social existence, the problem is exacerbated. It is possible that historical conditions compel African American practical theology to be, to a certain extent, anti-institutional, with regard to both the state and the church as sociopolitical entities.

One may ask whether African American theology lacks a social theory upon which to base its analysis of the problems of human society. Or one may ask whether African American theology is attentive to church organization. Both of these important questions point to an even larger, more comprehensive one: How is African American theology related to the sociopolitical problems of the world's poor and oppressed? This question as it is asked by people inside and outside of the African American churches, inside and outside of American society, constitutes the arena for African American practical theology.

For the African American practical theologian the problem of method centers around the issue of *social/cultural analysis.* This point has been critical for discussions among African American theologians. There is the further question of whether "blackness" or what W. E. B. Du Bois called the "Negro Problem" can provide within itself the critical and analytical methodology requisite for the task at hand. Cornel West has suggested that we need to combine a cultural and economic analysis, to understand the oppression of African Americans in particular, and the poor in general, in the world. Others sense a danger for African American theology in leaving a specifically cultural analysis for a transcultural one. The proliferation of perspectives makes it easy to see why the issue of method in African American practical theology is such a critical and crucial one. There is, however, one other aspect of this issue which should be taken into account. It is not uncommon to hear the assertion that criticism and analysis are not truly constitutive of theological method. The justification for this assertion is that neither cultural nor economic analysis is biblical or traditional. This position reveals, however, an unfortunate misunderstanding of the role of scripture and tradition within this theological task. In our view, by contrast, the Bible and tradition are seen as results of a particular, concrete analysis of the meaning of the revelation of God in the context of sociopolitical life, and the meaning of sociopolitical life emerges in the context of the revelation of God. The judgment that the African American practical theologian makes about the method of analysis, whether cultural, economic, or other, will not be based on some intrinsic quality of the method itself, but on whether that method helps us to understand the relation between the revelation of God and the sociopolitical context in which African Americans live.

The content of practical theology is a particular social problem. It is this content which energizes the theological task, and it is this aspect of theological reflection that is most likely to be seen as relevant to the life of the ordinary Christian. The epigraph that heads this chapter neatly summarizes why theology should be practical and problem-oriented. Yet it is difficult to convince theologians that social problems are proper issues for their attention and difficult to convince social theorists that there is any relation between social problems and the subject matter of theology. One observer notes that "expert opinion tends to regard social problems as technical matters to be addressed largely by technical means, and the elites of government, business, communications, education, the arts, and sciences only reluctantly engage in the kind of public discussion that matters most to Americans, discussions which consider the moral as well as the informational aspects of social issues."[7]

At the personal level the third task of African American theology then, along with fundamental and practical theology, is to examine the moral implications of Christian witness in the world. This witness itself involves three moral moments. First, Christians must engage in moral discernment; that is, Christians must look into the hearts of people, institutions, and social systems, to find the sources of impediments to justice and truth. Second, this moral discernment must be guided by moral norms. That is, one must have a set of criteria by which one can determine whether the present social order is just. Part of the difficulty here is finding a norm in the postmodern world, where the idea of norms is constantly called into question. Yet Christians are challenged to act and live in a way consistent with the deepest mandates of their faith. Third, the rules for Christian living should compel the believer to choose life, freedom, and integrity, and move the believer to action. Moral acts and moral existence are integrally related. Christians must act morally, but moral acts are grounded in a basic lifestyle and mindset that themselves are moral. Christians must exist as a moral people, but moral existence is buttressed by moral acts. Don S. Browning defines practical theology as "critical reflection on the church's dialogue with Christian sources and with other communities of experience and interpretation with the aim of guiding its action toward social and individual transformation."[8] The aim of the practical task of theology is the transformation of society and the individual. In the course of this transformation, however, theology itself is renewed. In the remainder of this chapter we will briefly review the concept of social problems and then relate this discussion to the notion of a theological problem. We will conclude with an analysis of "the Negro Problem" as both a social and a theological problem.

Social Problems as Theological Problems

A Conceptual Overview of Social Problems

The study of social problems has a long and fairly complex history. In one sense the notion of social problems or social issues evolved from the study of human society. From the period of the Protestant Reformation in the sixteenth century until the emergence of the discipline of sociology at the end of the nineteenth century, social problems were treated as part of the study of political economy. Here strictly religious or moral arguments for the alleviation of the symptoms of human misery were dominant. The challenge from churches to attend to the needs of the poor and the destitute was the foundation of a system of church-sponsored charity and social ministry. The latter decades of the nineteenth century and the opening decades of the twentieth century, however, gave rise to new explanatory paradigms for social problems. "It was not until the Charities Movement developed in Europe and the United States, e.g., 1860 to 1880, that literature in the sociology of social problems and social concern began to develop."[9] In particular the emergence of Darwinism provided both an explanation of and a suggested solution to a variety of social ills. One author writing in 1883 describes the similarity between the evolution of a species and the growth of a civilized society:

> Between the development of society and the development of species there is a close analogy. In the lowest forms of animal life there is little difference of part; both wants and powers are few and simple. . . . So homogeneous are some of these living things, that if cut in pieces, each piece still lives. But as life rises into higher manifestations, simplicity gives way to complexity. . . . In the ascending scale of life at last comes man, the most highly and delicately organized of animals. . . . But with man the ascending line stops. Animal life assumes no higher form; nor can we affirm that, in all his generations, man, as an animal, has a whit improved. But progression in another line begins. Where the development of species ends, social development commences.[10]

This view of society as the result of a continuous cycle of social improvements suggests that the social problems of hunger, poverty, homelessness, and the like are only temporary and that the growing social intelligence of the human race will render such problems extinct. Another explanatory paradigm for social problems was provided by the field of medicine. In that paradigm, society was viewed as an organism subject to various social pathologies. These problems or pathologies were treated and cured in order to restore social health.

5

With the emergence of the discipline of sociology, the study of social problems came to be understood as corollary of the study of society as a whole. However, sociology—the name is derived from the Latin *socius* (companion) and the Greek *logos* (science)—refers to a distinct field of study with its attendant methodologies. Like other disciplines, sociology sought to privilege methods of research and study that would compel its acceptance as a legitimate academic pursuit. Although, for a host of reasons, sociology was never able to divest itself completely of its amateur practitioners and sometimes pedantic devotees, it did finally come to be understood as science. The major difficulty that the emergence of sociology presented for the study of social problems is that the concept of social problems lacked a specific definition or a theoretical orientation. One writer notes that most books on social problems do not define their subject matter. While most will provide a short statement on the concept of social problems, these "brief definitions of social problems are so inadequate that some books on social problems do not even attempt to furnish definitions. This unfortunate situation has resulted from the fact that the selection of the particular social problems to be dealt with in sociology has been the result of accidental and historical developments rather than of strict logical divisions and distinctions. Because of this fact we do not find uniformity in the problems treated in the various social-problem texts, nor do we find entire agreement as to which belong to the domain of pure or general sociology rather than to applied sociology."[11] The fact that so many disparate social conditions were labeled as social problems resulted in definitions of social problems that were often strained and tautological:

> Defined succinctly, a social problem is an enduring, major community issue.... Defined in more detail, a social problem is ... a condition, real or imagined, judged undesirable by a considerable proportion of the members of a community ... judged by them to be a major threat to community life ... considered beyond the scope of, or uncontrollable by, traditional and formal norms ... considered capable of improvement through community action ... which becomes a general public issue and receives community-wide attention ... and about which there is enduring major controversy over what new norms to adopt.[12]

Besides the obvious semantic difficulties in the above statement, there is an absence of the precision needed to distinguished between genuine social problems and issues of generic social concern. The struggle here is to account for the both the subjective and the objective dimensions of what counts as a social problem. For example, it is possible that in one community the presence of vendors of sexually explicit material would be considered a social problem, while in another community it might not. Or it might be the case that the presence of only three such vendors in a community is not considered a social problem, while the addition of a fourth would be. In the following definition, the writer valiantly, but futilely, attempts to account for both the objective and subjective dimensions of social problems:

> A social problem is a condition which is defined by a considerable number of persons as a deviation from some social norm which they cherish. Every social problem thus consists of an objective condition and a subjective condition. The objective condition is a verifiable situation which can be checked as to existence and magnitude (proportions) by impartial and trained observers, e.g., the state of our national defense, trends in the birth rate, unemployment, etc. The subjective definition is the awareness of certain individuals that the condition is a threat to certain cherished values. . . . The objective condition is necessary but not in itself sufficient to constitute a social problem. . . . *Social problems are what people think they are* and if conditions are not defined as social problems by the problems involved in them, they are not problems to those people, although they may be problems to outsiders or to scientists. . . .[13]

Traditional definitions of social problems lacked coherence and precision and were filled with ambiguities. If social problems are what people think they are, to which people are we referring? What is the relation between a social problem and anything that offends one's moral sensibilities? In essence, social problems have been a label for a set of social conditions that have nothing in common other than they are called social problems. These social problems are a set of social conditions without a generic connection. "There is no overall theoretical orientation adequate to explain the existence or cause of all social problems. . . . 'No qualified sociologist holds that the discipline has evolved a single, strictly formulated theory that fully encompasses the wide range of social problems. . . . That sort of claim must be reserved to the pseudo sociologists who turn up in quantity whenever trouble is brewing in society and announce their quickly designed cures for everything that ails us socially.'"[14] Social problems are a collection of symptoms that to this point have escaped a comprehensive diagnosis.

One of the most significant developments in the study of social problems is the emergence of the constructivist view of social problems. In their important book, *Constructing Social Problems*, Malcolm Spector and John I. Kitsuse articulate a way of speaking of social problems that avoids the lack of clarity and precision which has characterized this field of study. They argue that social problems should not be thought of as a set of social conditions, for example, homelessness, poverty, or illiteracy. Instead:

> The notion that social problems are a kind of *condition* must be abandoned in favor of a conception of them as a kind of *activity*. We call this *claims-making activity*. . . . Our view is that any definition of social problems that begins "social problems are those conditions . . ." will lead to a conceptual and methodological impass that will frustrate attempts to build a specialized area of study. The question, then, is: if social problems cannot be conditions, what are they? Most succinctly, they are the activities of those who assert the existence of conditions and define them as social problems. . . . Thus, we define social problems as *the activities of individuals or groups making assertions of grievances and claims with respect to some putative conditions. . . . The central problem for a theory of social problems is to account for the emergence, nature, and maintenance of claims-making and responding activities. . . .* We are interested in constructing a theory of claims-making activities, not a theory of conditions. Thus, the significance of objective conditions for us is *the assertions made about them*, not the validity of those assertions as judged from some independent standpoint, as for example, that of a scientist.[15]

Spector and Kitsuse sought to lend clarity and precision to social problems research by shifting the focus away from the bewildering variety of social conditions that have been, are, or may be called social problems, and toward the common process of defining any set of conditions as social problems, that is, how these claims are made and by whom. The authors understandably overstate their case when they argue that whether the social conditions referred to actually exist is irrelevant. The point, however, is not to focus on the existence, extensiveness, or severity of a set of social conditions but on how those conditions come to be defined as social problems.

The process of defining social problems, in this view, centers on claims-making activities. "Claims-making is always a form of interaction: a demand made by one party to another that something be done about some putative condition. . . . All those who involve themselves in these activities participate in the process of defining social problems. . . . Claimants construct notions about the causes of the conditions they find onerous, assign blame, and locate officials responsible for rectifying the conditions."[16] In this view, values are important in defining social problems, but values, in and of themselves, are not the basis for defining a set of social conditions as a social problem. "The use of values to explain why people define social conditions as social problems is an explanation by fiat; it avoids addressing an important empirical issue, i.e., *how* and *by what process* do values produce such effects? . . . We observe people acting differently. We infer they have different values. Then we use these values to explain why they are acting differently."[17] Thus, the invocation of values is part of the process of defining a set of conditions as a social problem. (This is especially evident in the recent use of the term "family values." The term is used in making the claim that a set of imputed social conditions, for example, single-parent households and the cohabitation of unmarried persons, are a social problem.) Defined in this way, the naming of a social problem implies that a solution to that problem is attainable. In fact, one could argue that "solutions produce social problems by providing the framework within which those problems can be stated. . . . The belief that something could be done about a condition is a prerequisite to its becoming a social problem. People do not define as problems those conditions they feel are immutable, inherent in human nature, or the will of God."[18] This parallels one of the important distinctions which is made in theological discourse, between a problem and a mystery. A problem is soluble in the traditional sense of the term, while a mystery points to a more or less permanent and enduring depth dimension of human existence. Part of the task of practical theology is to distinguish between the two and to unmask attempts to reify existing social conditions by proclaiming them to be the mysterious will of God.

Social problems in this view cannot be defined either objectively or subjectively, because these options presume the existence of an external "ideal" against which social conditions are measured or an internal "ideal" against which all human assessments of social conditions are measured. By concerning ourselves with the claims-making process by which social problems come to be defined as such, we focus on the ways in which that process teaches all involved how to be social beings. Social problems are not the result of disagreements over the objective existence of certain social conditions, or disagreements over the subjective sentiments regarding those social conditions. They are the result of those rhetorical meaning-claims which shape the social dimensions of life itself. Thus the importance of this view of social problems for the task to be undertaken here is its emphasis on claims-making activities and rhetorical acts.

9

Theological Problems and Social Problems

An intricate, but often unnoticed, relationship exists between social problems and the ultimate questions of human existence. This relationship is sometimes obscured by assumptions that human problems are the domain of the human sciences while questions of ultimate concern are the province of theology. It is true that important distinctions are to be made between the aims and methods of sociology, psychology, and the like, and those of theology. Yet is also true that matters of ultimate concern are not so neatly separated into the holy and the mundane. This is especially true when a divine mandate is claimed for certain social arrangements. Attention to the ways that social problems manifest their theological dimensions and the ways that theological problems manifest their social dimensions will bring the practical theologian into the heart of the ultimate concerns of ordinary folk.

Theological problems are often associated with that which is ineffable, unfathomable, and mysterious. In many cases, the name given to that reality is God. Gordon Kaufman examined this aspect of religious thought in his book *God the Problem*. "The central problem of theological discourse, not shared with any other 'language game,' is the meaning of the term 'God.' 'God' raises special problems of meaning because it is a noun which by definition refers to a reality transcendent of, and thus not locatable within, experience."[19] Every theological problem refers in some way to God. Therefore, there is a sense in which one could say that God is a problem in human experience. In a more comprehensive sense, however, one could say that God refers to that dimension of human experience which escapes our attempts to grasp it. Seen from below, God is not the problem in human existence; rather, our understanding of human problems must be brought face to face with the God who accompanies us each day of our lives. It is this bringing of our problems face to face with the "God of our weary years" that introduces us again and again to the mystery that is God and also demystifies those problems. This is what is meant when African American Christians speak of "bringing everything to God in prayer" and "laying your burdens down at the feet of Jesus." Face to face with God, the theological dimensions of social problems are brought to light, and the social dimensions of theological problems become apparent.

In his more recent book, *In Face of Mystery: A Constructive Theology*, Kaufman attempts to unravel the meaning of mystery in theological discourse. He argues that mystery has a fundamentally intellectual character, whatever its experiential overtones. It refers to bafflement of mind more than obscurity of perception. A mystery is something we find we cannot think clearly about, cannot get our minds around, cannot manage to grasp. . . . But to say "It is a mystery" does not yet tell us anything specific about the subject matter we are seeking to grasp or understand. "Mystery" is, rather, a grammatical or linguistic operator by means of which we remind ourselves of something about ourselves: that at this point we are using our language in an unusual, limited, and potentially misleading way.[20]

Mystery refers to the processes and limits of our thinking and speaking rather than to the objects of our thought. Mystery is the name we give to our ongoing attempts to find meaning in and solutions to those human problems that appear to be timeless, permanent, novel, contemporary, but always intractable. Kaufman notes that

Every religious tradition of which we know grew up over many generations in connection with the basic activities of everyday living and dying. . . . Over the course of time, in each growing tradition, certain modes of thinking and acting, of meditation and practice, proved increasingly helpful in diagnosing and defining some of the more difficult problems and ills faced by the society, thus making available treatments and remedies that were healing and in other ways effective. . . . The world-pictures which became central to the religion . . . were at first not in any way specifically or distinctly "religious" in our modern sense. . . . These human images and ideas of the world have always been the product of human imaginings in face of the wide range of problems confronted in life, the "imaginative construction" of pictures which made some sense of life by setting it in a wider and deeper context, thus facilitating (more or less) effective address of the problems which it posed.[21]

Human problems, or social problems, are theological problems because they bring us face to face with the ultimate questions of human existence. In seeking to "have life and to have it more abundantly" we are not only concerned with the activities of getting and spending. We are also concerned with the meaning of life itself. This is the reason that it is perfectly appropriate and even necessary to make social problems the subject of theological reflection. This reflection is always both critical and constructive:

The world in which we live, thus, cannot be conceived any longer simply as a given structure which women and men must accept precisely as it is. In many respects it is plastic to our interests and purposes; we have the freedom and power to make it into something that it at present is not. To what extent do we have such freedom and power? To what extent are we constrained by orders and powers completely beyond our control? And in what respects *should* we attempt to transform further the world in which we live, and the structure of human existence itself? All these questions require address if we are to be properly oriented in life today.[22]

There are certainly limits to human agency in the world, and evil does exist in the world. Yet we will discover the limits of human agency only by working as though they do not exist. We will recognize the power of evil only by seeking to do good in the world. Therefore we must critically question any and all attempts to convince us to accept any given social arrangement by appealing to mystery. We must be continually tenacious in our quest for solutions to the problems that plague our society. In a speculative sense, the idea of God may present itself as an intellectual problem. Yet, in a practical sense, God is not the problem. God is the answer.

Further reflection on claims-making can clarify religion's social roles and character. In a groundbreaking work, *The Nature of Doctrine: Religion and Theology in a Postliberal Age*, George A. Lindbeck takes up the question of doctrinal disagreement.[23] In the context of ecumenical discussion, Lindbeck examines the sometimes shallow, often limited, results of attempts at doctrinal reconciliation. He identifies two ways of conceptualizing religion that he believes exacerbate rather than solve certain theological problems. These he calls the "cognitivist" and the "experiential-expressive":

> One of these emphasizes the cognitive aspects of religion and stresses the ways in which church doctrines function as informative propositions or truth claims about objective realities. . . . A second approach focuses on what I shall call . . . the "experiential-expressive" dimension of religion, and it interprets doctrines as noninformative and nondiscursive symbols of inner feelings, attitudes, or existential orientations.[24]

Lindbeck argues that these dominant ways of thinking about religion do not contribute substantively to resolving disagreement among conflicting religious and theological positions. Religion or theology as a special body of knowledge has been difficult to defend since the Enlightenment. Claims to superior knowledge are not ultimately persuasive in resolving theological conflict or problems. Being religious, while it may involve familiarity with a certain body of knowledge (tradition), certainly involves more than knowing. On the other hand, religion, understood as comprised of feelings, attitudes, and existential orientations, is more tolerant of differences among persons. Rather than leading to the resolution of theological conflicts and problems, however, this view of religion permits only shallow empathy among competing perspectives. Being religious, while it may involve certain feelings and attitudes (piety), certainly involves more than feeling. Lindbeck argues for an understanding of religions that sees them as types of cultural-linguistic systems incorporating both cognitive and experiential-expressive elements. In this view:

> Religions are seen as comprehensive interpretive schemes, usually embodied in myths or narratives and heavily ritualized, which structure human experience and understanding of self and world. . . . [A religion] is similar to an idiom that makes possible the description of realities, the formulation of beliefs, and the experiencing of inner attitudes, feelings and sentiments. Like a culture or language, it is a communal phenomenon that shapes the subjectivities of individuals rather than being primarily a manifestation of those subjectivities. . . . Its doctrines, cosmic stories or myths, and ethical directives are integrally related to the rituals it practices, the sentiments or experiences it evokes, the actions it recommends, and the institutional forms it develops.[25]

The value of this perspective is that it allows us to understand how and under what circumstances theological conflicts and problems can be understood and resolved. In this view the truth-claims of a religion are governed by the language system of that religion, but they are also creative responses to a changing environment:

> Thus while a religion's truth claims are often of the utmost importance to it (as in the case of Christianity), it is, nevertheless, the conceptual vocabulary and the syntax or inner logic which determine the kinds of truth claims the religion can make. The cognitive aspect, while often important, is not primary. . . . The first-order truth claims of a religion change insofar as these arise from the application of the interpretive scheme to the shifting worlds that human beings inhabit. What is taken to be reality is in large part socially constructed and consequently alters in the course of time. . . . To the degree that religions are like languages, they can obviously remain the same amid vast transformations of affirmation and experience.[26]

The importance of the claims that a religion makes about the nature of reality lies more in the act of making the claim than in the specific content of the claim itself. For in making such claims we learn how to be religious. In becoming religious "one learns how to feel, act, and think in conformity with a religious tradition that is, in its inner structure, far richer and more subtle than can be explicitly articulated. The primary knowledge is not *about* the religion, nor *that* the religion teaches such and such, rather *how* to be religious in such and such ways."[27] Since one cannot adequately understand the function of religion by appealing to some common body of propositional knowledge or to some notion of common human experience, religious or theological problems must be seen in the context of the rhetorical process by which claims about the nature of ultimate reality are made. In this way theological problems have an inherently social character. The cultural-linguistic model "understands religions as idioms for dealing with whatever is most important—with ultimate questions of life and death, right and wrong, chaos and order, meaning and meaninglessness. These are the problems they treat in their stories, myths, and doctrines. . . . Different religions seem in many cases to produce fundamentally divergent depth experiences of what it is to be human."[28] In essence, theological problems are not the result of cognitive disagreement or experiential-expressive dissonance. They are the result of differing grammars, languages, stories, and truth-claims that shape the religious dimensions of life itself.

The Negro Problem

Nearly one hundred years ago W. E. B. Du Bois observed that "the problem of the twentieth century is the problem of the color line—the relation of the darker to the lighter races of men in Asia and Africa, in America and the islands of the sea."[29] Du Bois, more than any thinker before or since his time, examined, sometimes in minute detail, all of the facets of "the Negro Problem." He viewed the entirety of American history since the end of the Civil War as preoccupied with the issue of the presence and place America's African population. As a sociologist, Du Bois clearly understood the "Negro Problem" to be a social problem. Issues of employment, education, housing, and health of African Americans were at the heart of many of Du Bois's writings. Yet Du Bois also knew that the Negro Problem was more than a riddle to be solved by a more equitable distribution of the nation's riches. A review of the literature reveals a host of works that focus on the Negro Problem as a social problem. The common thread in these works is that they focus on only one aspect of the problem; that is, what shall be done with, to, and for the African in America.[30] What they neglect is the relation between what C. Wright Mills called "personal troubles" and "public issues." Mills observed that

Social Problems as Theological Problems

Troubles occur within the character of the individual and within the range of his immediate relations with others; they have to do with his self and with those limited areas of social life of which he is directly and personally aware. Accordingly, the statement and the resolution of troubles properly lie within the individual as a biographical entity and within the scope of his immediate milieu—the social setting that is directly open to his personal experience and to some extent his willful activity. A trouble is a private matter. . . . *Issues* have to do with matters that transcend these local environments of the individual and the range of his inner life. They have to do with the organization of many such milieux into the institutions of an historical society as a whole, with the ways in which various milieus overlap and interpenetrate to form the larger structure of social and historical life. An issue is a public matter.[31]

In a particularly poetic and introspective passage in *The Souls of Black Folk*, Du Bois examines the personal experience of being a problem:

Between me and the other world there is ever an unasked question: unasked by some through feelings of delicacy; by others through the difficulty of rightly framing it. All, nevertheless, flutter round it. They approach me in a half-hesitant sort of way, eye me curiously or compassionately, and then, instead of saying directly, How does it feel to be a problem? . . . At these I smile, or am interested, or reduce the boiling to a simmer, as the occasion may require. To the real question, How does it feel to be a problem? I seldom answer a word. And yet, being a problem is a strange experience,—peculiar even for one who has never been anything else, save perhaps in babyhood and in Europe.[32]

There are few, if any, other groups in the history of the West who have been more often characterized as "a problem" than African Americans. In a racialized culture, social problems take on a distinctive cast. Du Bois describes the personal dimensions of the Negro Problem as a striving to overcome a "double-consciousness"—a sense of "twoness," an internal conflict in the soul of African Americans, the solution to which is as difficult to attain as the solution to the external conflict within the body politic engendered by their presence.[33] Further, Du Bois also understood that the Negro Problem is also a theological problem, as his writings on the black church and black religion show. Du Bois saw the Negro Problem as both objective and subjective, focusing on both fact and feeling. If the problem is one of ignorance, then the solution is education. If the problem is one of intolerance, then the solution is conversion. When the race problem is discussed, most often one of these two paradigmatic frameworks is employed.

Interestingly, they correspond to classical "liberal" and "orthodox" notions of salvation. The Negro Problem, however, as a social problem, has not been solved by appealing to more education (for either European Americans or African Americans). Fannie Barrier Williams, a contemporary of Du Bois, in a 1905 essay described being a "colored girl" in light of the Negro Problem: "That the term 'colored girl' is almost a term of reproach in the social life of America is all too true; she is not known and hence not believed in; she belongs to a race that is best designated by the term 'problem,' and she lives beneath the shadow of that problem which envelopes and obscures her."[34]

The Negro Problem, as a theological problem, has not been solved by appealing to progressive revelation or cataclysmic personal conversion (on the part of either European Americans or African Americans). In essence, the Negro Problem is not the result of the ignorance of European Americans or of their intolerance of the presence of African Americans. It is the result of the clash between two different cultural-linguistic systems. As Du Bois implies, black people and white people in the West inhabit two different worlds, separated by a veil. The heart of the Negro Problem, as a social problem, he claimed, is the claim to be both "an American [and] a Negro; two souls, two thoughts, two unreconciled strivings; two warring ideals in one dark body, whose dogged strength alone keeps it from being torn asunder."[35] From a Christian theological perspective, the heart of the Negro Problem is the claim to be both black and Christian, with all the attendant ambiguities and conflicts. The cultural-linguistic system in which African Americans live serves a variety of purposes. It orients them in an often hostile and indifferent environment. Yet it also provides a strong line of defense, protecting that creative spark that continues to make black life liveable. It is both constructive and deconstructive at the same time. Toni Morrison notes that the one feature which distinguishes a work of literature as "black" is found in its use of language: "What makes a work 'Black'? The most valuable point of entry into the question of cultural (or racial) distinction, the one most fraught, is its language—its unpoliced, seditious, confrontational, manipulative, inventive, disruptive, masked and unmasking language."[36]

The chapters that follow are preliminary attempts to understand three of the more persistent and intractable social problems of our time. The thesis that guides these examinations is that every genuine social problem is, at bottom, a theological problem. Framing the discussions in ways that are sometimes obvious and often subtle, is the assumption that somewhere beneath the surface lurks some form of the Negro Problem.

Honor, Shame, and Grace

Amazing grace, how sweet the sound,
that saved a wretch like me.
I once was lost, but now I'm found,
was blind, but now I see.
—John Newton

One of the most critical problems facing the African American community today is the lack of self-esteem and its attendant maladies. The history of African people in the Western world has resulted in an inexorable chipping away at their collective self-worth. True, the issue is certainly not the exclusive domain of African peoples in the New World. The advent of industrialization and massive bureaucratic and economic structures has done much to cast a long shadow over the question of the worth of the human being in general. Yet, for a variety of reasons the issue of self-esteem has been persistent in the experience of African Americans, and the resources available to them for addressing the issue have been limited.

To put the matter more bluntly, one might say that the self-esteem of African Americans has historically been and continues to be under assault. This assault is most often supported and enhanced by the rhetorical structures and conceptual frameworks of honor and shame. Lack of self-esteem is rooted in the experience of being dishonored. The sense of dishonor is related to and in many ways grounded in the social dislocation of African slaves during the Middle Passage. It continues to reappear in the deep sense of loss felt as poor black men, women, and children negotiate the impersonal labyrinth of the social welfare system. This dishonor is not limited to black persons of lower socioeconomic status. In many important respects it is an acutely felt dimension of the life experience of middle-class and upper-income African Americans, especially as they move into the "white space" of the corporate and professional world. Although the terms "honor" and "shame" are rarely, if ever, used to describe the problem itself, it will become apparent that they exert tremendous influence on the way in which human beings are affirmed and valued in our society.

The central concern of this chapter is to examine the theological underpinnings of this problem. The purpose is to contribute to our ability to do theology and ministry taking seriously the particular dynamics of human valuation, specifically those of honor and shame, which permeate our society. The thesis which guides this discussion is that notions of honor and shame as more or less persistent categories of social order and ordering are crucial in the articulation of an African American theology of grace.

Since the language of honor and shame is seldom directly employed in discourse on human social problems, we will begin with an illustration of how these rhetorical strategies are employed in the argument against those policies and programs known collectively as affirmative action. A conceptual overview of the major scholarly discussions of honor and shame in the field of cultural anthropology will provide the context for a brief examination of the influence of these concepts in the enslavement of Africans in the New World. Additionally, it will be important to ask how the rhetorical strategies of honor and shame function in the Bible, before concluding with a proposal for the articulation of an African American doctrine of grace.

The Affirmative Action Debate: The Rhetoric of Honor and Shame

The term "affirmative action" refers to a group of policies and procedures which began with Title VII of the Civil Rights Act of 1964. The original purpose of Title VII was to ensure fair employment practices for person whose race, gender, religion, or nationality might be used against them. In spite of the broad net cast by the original language, these policies and procedures became the flashpoint for discussions around remedies for past wrongs done to African Americans. Although they were the law of the land, these policies were not embraced by everyone. Many felt, and feel even more strongly today, that such preferential treatment of black people reduces the opportunities for employment and education for more "qualified" white persons. "Reverse discrimination" suits are now numerous.

Within that cacophony of voices, however, there were and are some who object to affirmative action, not on the basis of its presumed deleterious effects on white people but on its purported effect on black self-esteem. This group, which includes some highly visible black conservative writers, are not monolithic in their reasoning, but they share a common refrain. That is, they argue that attempts to level the playing field in employment and education actually do a disservice to black people because they contribute to the sense of black shame and dishonor. An illustration will suffice to make the point. In their controversial book, *The Bell Curve: Intelligence and Class Structure in American Life*, Richard J. Herrnstein and Charles Murray present a detailed argument on intelligence and race that is seriously flawed in both its assumptions and methodology. More important to this discussion is their critique of affirmative action programs. For them the central question regarding these programs in universities is, "How much harm is done to minority self-esteem, to white perceptions of minorities, and ultimately to ethnic relations by a system that puts 'academically less able' minority students side by side with students who are more able?"[1] The issue here is not the validity of their claims but the rhetorical strategies they employ to make their case. They point out that when so-called nonqualified black students are placed on campuses with white students, white students will resent these black ones because "they don't belong there." Black students will feel the sting of white approbation and become ashamed. The authors imply that this shaming is the cause of high dropout rates among black college students on white campuses. And even black students who do survive and graduate never receive the status which would ordinarily accrue to them as holders of a degree, because "people will know" that they did not earn it, but were "simply granted" a degree because of affirmative action. That is, they will never enjoy the "honor" that is due them. Similar observations can be made about the objections to affirmative action programs in the workplace. Here the black worker who receives employment opportunities which ought to, presumably, have gone to a white worker, will suffer the shame of doing inferior work and never receive the deserved honor of any position he or she occupies in the workplace. The conservative African American writer, Shelby Steele, in his book *The Content of Our Character*, for example, argues that affirmative action programs contribute to a demoralization of black people by enlarging their self-doubt.[2] In an even more poignant way, Steele points to the atavistic response of white people to black people and the resulting feeling of shame that often follows. This shame is the result of a negative evaluation of black people in the eyes of white persons.

In essence, affirmative action is wrong, according to this view, because it exposes black people to the shame of being the lesser among equals and prevents those who believe that they merit honor from receiving it. The fallacy of this reasoning is summarized by Cornel West. He observes that black conservatives desperately desire the approval of their white colleagues and will deny that racism in any way impedes their success as a way of cementing their relationship with their white counterparts. "The need of black conservatives to gain the respect of their white peers deeply shapes certain elements of their conservatism."[3] They want to be judged as others are judged and therefore oppose affirmative action programs. The double irony is that these very programs are largely responsible for their entry into the middle class, and that, in spite of their efforts, "genuine white peer acceptance still seems to escape them."

Honor and shame are more or less universal conceptual categories in human existence. Affirmative action programs have benefited white women, Hispanics, and other ethnic groups. However, what is curious is that just as affirmative action has come to mean doing something primarily for black people, the notions of honor and shame have been critically, and almost exclusively, refracted through the lens of race in our culture. Before we move on to a discussion of the relationship of these concerns to an African American doctrine of grace, a brief conceptual overview of recent scholarly discussion of honor and shame in cultural anthropology is in order.

A Conceptual Overview of Honor and Shame

Honor and shame have been recognized as categories of human evaluation as early as the rise of Greco-Roman culture. These themes have been latent or manifest in almost every historical period and in every society. Yet their importance in the broad scheme of social evaluation and ordering in the modern era first received systematic attention in the 1950s, when a group of cultural anthropologists gathered to discuss the significance of their field work among Mediterranean societies. The researchers discovered that certain systems of thought that undergirded particular systems of social ordering and evaluation were common to all of the societies studied. They found that

> honour and shame are social evaluations and thus participate in the nature of social sanctions. . . . Honour and shame are two poles of an evaluation. They are the reflection of the social personality in the mirror of social ideals. What is particular to these evaluations is that they use as a standard of measurement the type of personality considered as representative and exemplary of a certain society. . . . Honour is at the apex of the pyramid of temporal social values and it conditions their hierarchical order. Cutting across all other social classifications it divides social beings into two fundamental categories, those endowed with honour and those deprived of it. . . . This way of reasoning can only lead to the conclusion that as all societies evaluate conduct by comparing it to the ideal standards of action, all societies have their own forms of honour and shame.[4]

While these early studies focused on one particular set of societies, further research has shown that the notions of honor and shame exert a powerful influence on the societies of southern Europe, particularly Spain, Italy, and France. In these societies, the discourse of honor and shame are woven into the very fabric of the culture. That does not mean, however, that notions of honor and shame are not powerful influences in other societies. As one author notes, "It has been frequently remarked from early times that those people who make most use of the words 'honour' and 'shame' and others associated with them in ordinary conversation, are not those whose lives are most strictly governed by the principles which those words express."[5] So even when the language of honor and shame is not manifest in a given culture, it may still function in a powerful though latent manner to influence social evaluation of human conduct.

The literature on honor and shame is plentiful, complex, and broad. It ranges from etymological studies on the words for honor in Spanish, Italian, and French literatures, to the patterns of domestic organization in Middle Eastern peasant societies. The ideas of honor and shame have intermittently emerged as subjects for the discipline of ethics (see Aristotle's *Ethics*), philosophy (see David Hume's "The Rise of Arts and Sciences"), sociology (see Peter Berger's essay "On the Obsolescence of the Concept of Honour") and political theory (see Thomas Hobbes' *Leviathan*).[6] But in all of these disciplines a certain ambiguity surrounds the notions of honor and shame. The ambiguity centers on the question whether honor and shame are moral categories or political forces. Cultural anthropological studies valuably set aside the question whether the forms of honor and shame in a given society fit into preexisting cognitive frameworks. In spite of the always warranted caveat regarding the bias which the researcher brings to scientific observation, this rich and fertile area of research yields several themes and a conceptual framework for our central thesis.

In one of the more succinct analyses of these concepts of honor and shame, one of its pioneers, Julian Pitt-Rivers, offers the following summary of the meaning of honor:

> The notion of honor has several facets. It is a sentiment, a manifestation of this sentiment in conduct, and the evaluation of this conduct by others, that is to say, reputation. It is both internal to the individual and external to him—a matter of his feelings, his behavior, and the treatment that he receives. . . . Honor expresses an evaluation of self in the terms which are used to evaluate others—or as others might be imagined to judge one. It can, therefore, be seen to reflect the values of the group with which a person identifies himself. But honor as a fact, rather than as a sentiment, refers not merely to the judgement of others but to their behavior. The facets of honor may be viewed as related in the following way: honor felt becomes honor claimed, and honor claimed becomes honor paid. The payment of honor involves the expression of respect which is due to a person either by virtue of his role on a particular occasion . . . or by virtue of his status or rank. . . . The withdrawal of respect dishonors, since it implies a rejection of the claim to honor and this inspires the sentiment of shame. To be put to shame is to be denied honor, and it follows that this can only be done to those who have some pretension to it. He who makes no such claim has nothing to lose. . . . Those who aspire to no honor cannot be humiliated. . . . Hence, honor is not only the internalization of the values of society in the individual but the externalization of his self-image in the world.[7]

Honor, then, is a means by which an individual assesses whether or not he or she has attained the ideals prescribed by the society of which he or she desires to be a part. It provides "a nexus between the ideals of a society and their reproduction in the individual through his (or her) aspiration to personify them."[8]

The first major theme that emerges in the literature on honor and shame is their rootedness in social structures. "Because honor must always be given by someone *to* someone else, it is inescapably social—and thus depends on norms which are socially acknowledged."[9] In Hellenistic societies, honor and shame were associated with the status that accompanied one's social standing relative to the aristocracy and ultimately to the Emperor. In most monarchies honor and shame were associated with one's social standing relative to the crown. "Medieval society was ranked in terms of honor, from the aristocracy, who had the most—on account of their power, their valor, and their proximity to the king—to those who had none at all, the heretics and the outcasts, those who indulged in infamous occupations or had been convicted of infamy."[10] In these cases, honor could be inherited by virtue of a noble birth, or ascribed, by virtue of meritorious conduct. Following the Middle Ages, honor and shame were associated with one's social standing relative to the landed aristocracy. In this latter manifestation, the social codes of honor and shame "came to define the lives of gentlemen both in Europe and in the American South. . . . [This was especially evident in] the glorification of dueling in both European and Southern codes of honor."[11] In essence, honor and shame were rooted in social structures where stratification and inequality were the order of the day.

The primacy of honor and shame as modes of social organization is often related to the absence of commonly accepted legal structures in a given group or society. Honor was "a pseudo legal institution governing the sphere of social etiquette where the law was either not competent or not welcome."[12] This is why the customs of the joust and the duel in their respective eras were so difficult to erase. This relation between honor and the absence of effective legal restrictions explains why codes of honor are most obvious among urban gangs, street corner societies, the military, paramilitary organizations, prison populations, organized crime families, and the very wealthy, among others. What these groups have in common is that they exist either outside of or above the law. They tend to regulate themselves, and are, for all practical purposes, *a law unto themselves.*[13]

The second major theme to emerge from the study of honor and shame is the relation between honor and power. The seventeenth-century English philosopher Thomas Hobbes argues in his work *Leviathan* that honor is simply one of those scarce goods for which human beings are locked in battle. Thus it is only by force that one can attain and retain honor. Indeed, it seems that one only has honor if one has the capacity to defend it. This is why honor, in this context, is related to the physical person. It is by physical force that one demonstrates the willingness to defend one's honor. "The ultimate vindication of honour lies in physical violence and when other means fail the obligation exists, not only in the formal code of honour, but in social milieux which admit no such code, to revert to it."[14] In the final analysis, when all else fails, one must employ violence to defend one's honor and to avoid dishonor.

The third major theme related to honor and shame is the role of gender in their manifestation in a given culture. Julian Pitt-Rivers notes that

> Male and female honor are clearly differentiated with regard to conduct. A moral division of labor operates within the family, especially in the Latin countries: the aspect of honor as precedence becomes, according to this system of values, the prerogative of the male, while honor as sexual purity is restricted to the female. Hence, sexual conquest enhances the prestige of men; sexual liberty defiles the honor of women. (Congruently, a high value is attached to virginity in unmarried girls.) The defense of female purity, however, is a male responsibility, and men are therefore vulnerable to dishonor not through their own sexual misconduct but through that of their womenfolk—that is to say, members of the same nuclear family, including mother, wife, unmarried sister, and daughter. Hence, sexual insults that impugn the honor of men refer not to them but to their women.[15]

The irony of this situation is that a condition of social conflict is set up by the contradictory nature of the requirements of honor for women and men. Women, in this context, can avoid dishonor by displaying the attributes of humility and deference. A woman's honor, however, is only guaranteed by the efforts of her male protectors. At the same time, a man's honor cannot, in this instance, be impugned by his own sexual indiscretions. In fact, his honor is upheld to the degree that he is successful in the sexual conquests of other women, and thus, in the dishonoring of her male relatives. The symbolic representation of male superiority in this battle for honor is centered on the male genitalia—and more especially, the testicles (*cajones*) in certain southern European cultures. They become the sign of manliness and honor. A curious and revealing twist to this insight is that where the social roles of men and women are abrogated, the notions of honor and shame collapse. "Once the sexual division of labour breaks down, women become men and where this occurs there can be neither honour nor shame. . . . A woman stripped of her honour becomes a man."[16] Conversely, a man who is dishonored—especially by virtue of an inability to defend the women of his family or by his low social status—is himself thought of as a woman.

In essence, because a man may be dishonored by the conquest of his woman by another man, he must protect her. Because a man may be dishonored by the exercise of sexual liberty by his woman, he must enforce a system of social control which limits her opportunities. Because a woman can pretend to no honor of her own, the best that she can hope for is to avoid the appearance of dishonorable conduct.

The fourth observation to be made concerning honor and shame is that shame is not merely the absence of honor. They are, rather, two ends of a spectrum that defines the range of human evaluation. There is, in this conception, no neutral state of being without honor. One either has honor, or one is shamed. Shame, therefore, like honor, has its own set of cultural markers and social stigmata. Shame is most often related to what I call "a rhetoric of loss." This kind of discourse accompanies the realization that one exists in a state of shame. In his classic work, *A Theory of Justice*, John Rawls describes honor or self-esteem that is related to the esteem in which one is held by others, as a primary human good. He uses the language of loss to describe shame. "Now we may characterize shame as the feeling that someone has when he experiences an injury to his self-respect or suffers a blow to his self-esteem. Shame is painful since it is the loss of a prized good."[17] In fact, it is the rhetoric of loss that distinguishes guilt from shame. "In the one [guilt] we focus on the infringement of the just claims of others and the injury we have done to them, and on their probable resentment or indignation should they discover our deed. Whereas in the other [shame] we are struck by the loss to our self-esteem and our inability to carry out our aims: we sense the diminishment of self from our anxiety about the lesser respect that others may have for us and from our disappointment with ourself for failing to live up to our ideals."[18] Silvan Tomkins, a research psychologist, focuses on the relationship between shame and human neurobiological processes. He notes that "shame is felt as an inner torment, a sickness of the soul. . . . [The person shamed] feels himself naked, defeated, alienated, lacking in dignity or worth."[19] Here again shame is associated with a rhetoric of loss. For Tomkins, to be shamed is to *lose face*. "How can loss of face be more intolerable than loss of life? How can hanging the head in shame so mortify the spirit?" he asks. "In contrast to all other affects, shame is an experience of the self by the self. At that moment when the self feels ashamed, it is felt as a sickness within the self. Shame is the most reflexive of affects in that the phenomenological distinction between the subject and object of shame is lost."[20] In his fascinating analysis of the relationship between shame and contempt, Tomkins notes that while shame does involve the loss of intimacy and communion between "the self and the self," as well as "the self and others," this loss is not permanent. This loss is only made permanent (and I would argue, therefore tragic) by *contempt*:

Whenever an individual, a class, or a nation wishes to maintain a hierarchical relationship, or to maintain aloofness it will have to resort to contempt of the other. Contempt is the mark of the oppressor. The hierarchical relationship is maintained either when the oppressed one assumes the attitude of contempt for himself or hangs his head in shame. In the latter case he holds on to the oppressor as an identification object with whom he can aspire to mutuality, in whom he can be interested, whose company he can enjoy, with the hope that the oppressor will on occasion be interested in him. If, however, the predominant interaction is one of contempt from superior to inferior, and the inferior internalizes the affect of contempt and hangs his head in contempt from the self as well as contempt from the oppressor, then it is more accurate to say that the oppressor has also taught the oppressed to have contempt for themselves rather than to be ashamed of themselves. In a democratically organized society the belief that all men are created equal means that all men are possible objects of identification. When one man expresses contempt for another, the other is more likely to experience shame than self-contempt insofar as the democratic ideal has been internalized. . . . Contempt will be used sparingly in a democratic society lest it undermine solidarity, whereas it will be used frequently and with approbation in a hierarchically organized society in order to maintain distance between individuals, classes, and nations.[21]

In sum, shame is associated with loss, but not permanent loss. Contempt is associated with permanent loss. Shame is associated with democratic social structures, in which the bonds of intimacy and communion, while attenuated, are never actually broken. Contempt is associated with hierarchical social structures that depend on unbridgeable chasms between individuals, classes, and nations.

The rhetoric of loss as the discourse of shame can also be seen in broader collective terms. Julio Caro Baroja argues that notions of honor and shame during the Spanish Inquisition were related to the idea of racial purity or "purity of blood." During this period "the whole of Spain was dominated by a preoccupation with the concepts of 'purity' and 'cleanliness of blood' and of 'impurity', 'stain' or 'blot'; this 'purity of blood' being equated with 'honour', and 'impurity' with 'dishonour.'"[22] Thus shame was associated with having Jewish blood as opposed to "Gothic" blood. In a larger context, shame is, in this instance, defined by discourse which speaks of the loss of racial purity.

The rhetoric of loss is both the mark of the ones who are shamed and their way of ameliorating the effects of shame. To speak of one's loss is to confirm immediately one's dishonor, because one has lost control of the situation and of one's emotions. One writer has argued that women and other social outsiders have perfected the rhetoric of loss, because the means to attain honor have been denied to them. Along with women, Lila Abu-Lughod argues, "mad people, idiots, and children who also express the experiences of loss in an uncontrolled way are considered outside society in some sense—they are not fully social beings or proper members of society. Ineffectual and dependent, they have no honor."[23] This rhetoric of loss most often takes the form of poetry, song, or some other artistic vehicle that offers a socially acceptable means of expression while providing a way of warding off the death-dealing effects of shame, social dislocation, and powerlessness.

Many of the particular social conditions that have been described above may appear inapplicable to contemporary society. Precedence, in modern Western societies, is accorded on the basis of economics; women are, generally, more independent than these descriptions suggest, and the avenues for winning honor through physical courage have been largely limited to sports and war.[24] Although the context has changed, however, the principles of honor and shame remain as constant and universal social structures of human evaluation. Both the constancy and complexity of these social structures are evident in the historical experience of African slaves and their descendants in the New World. What follows is a brief discussion of some of the ways that honor and shame can assist in understanding what challenges were presented to African Americans and what responses were required of African Americans by the institution of slavery. From this analysis it may be possible to understand how these structures continue to influence black life.

Honor, Shame, and American Slavery

Historian Orlando Patterson has noted that the American South in the eighteenth and nineteenth centuries was an honor and shame culture.[25] Indeed, he argues that the economic motives for the enslavement of Africans were minimal and paled in comparison to the value of the slave in confirming the honor of the slavemaster. In Patterson's view, the primary purpose of slavery was to impute honor to those who held slaves. This meant that slaves and slaveholders were held together within an Hegelian dialectic of dependency and submission. (I would agree that the requirement of honor was a large part of the system of slavery but not to the total exclusion of the economic benefits to the slaveholder.) Slavocracy in the South was a society unto itself, with its own laws, codes, and symbolic points of reference. The highly stratified character of Southern society, its codes of male chivalry and female reticence, meant that the structures of honor and shame were more pronounced there than in other parts of the United States. Moreover, notions of honor and shame can provide a way of understanding the attempts of African American slaves to navigate their environment in light of their reading and misreading of the social script of racial oppression. Patterson argues that "the dishonor which the slave was compelled to experience sprang . . . from that raw human sense of debasement inherent in having no being except as an expression of another's being."[26] I would argue, however, that the imputation of shame onto slaves within the system of slavery was meant both to counter the aspirations of African slaves to honor and to prove that they were dishonorable.

Shame rather than guilt is the operative emotional response in this instance. The puritanical notion of guilt was a central component in the American religious psyche of the eighteenth and nineteenth centuries, and it received its most striking treatment in Nathaniel Hawthorne's novel *The Scarlet Letter*. The sexual liaison between Reverend Mr. Arthur Dimmesdale and Miss Hester Prynne expressed allegorically the preoccupation of a certain segment of American society with the guilt brought on by sin. As Hawthorne deftly notes, guilt has no natural external manifestation. This is why Hester Prynne was made to wear the scarlet letter *A* on her clothing. In a striking twist of the plot, the same letter mysteriously appears on the chest of Reverend Dimmesdale. The point here is that the effects of guilt are usually private and individual, while the effects of shame are public and social. Because African slaves came from African social contexts of honor and shame, the puritanical notion of guilt was not as significant to them. The idea of shame, however, was an effective means of social control.

For the purposes of this discussion, three observations can be made regarding the effects of the honor and shame codes on African slaves. First, because slaves came from traditional societies that had their own codes of honor and shame, many of them sought to accommodate to this new social context by drawing on their cultural memory. They understood from the practices of slavery within traditional African societies that to be a slave was to be shamed or dishonored. But they also understood that the effects of shame could be mitigated in several ways. They could seek honor in limited ways through meritorious conduct. By faithfully serving their masters, they might merit a measure of honor. They could seek honor by claiming it as their birthright. Some slaves did claim honor because their fathers were white. The tragic dimension to this claim is that it usually required shaming their mothers, and these claims to paternally rooted honor were usually denied. Or they could seek honor as slaves did in ancient Greco-Roman culture, by situating themselves as close as possible to the source and fount of honor, the white slaveholder. This is the root of the form of classism prevalent on some plantations which made distinctions between "field hands," who labored far from the master's mansion, and the "house servants," who enjoyed proximity to the center of power. These ways to honor were the only avenues open to slaves because exercising physical force or violence to attain or retain one's honor often carried too great a cost. In the final analysis, every avenue to honor exercised by African slaves was eventually revealed to be a dead end because African slaves were actually excluded from the honor and shame culture of the South. African slaves were not simply regarded as shamed persons but were, recalling the insights of Silvan Tomkins, held in contempt. This notion of *contempt* as opposed to *shame* was what distinguished the enslavement of Africans in the modern world from every prior form of human enslavement. Being held in contempt was the epitome of human alienation.

Second, honor and shame in American slavery were associated with sexuality. Since the honor of women was symbolized by their chastity, black women in slavery could aspire to no honor because their sexual purity was constantly compromised by the rapacious sexual appetites of their slavemasters. Moreover, black men were dishonored because of their inability to defend their wives, sisters, daughters, and mothers from sexual assault. At the same time, myths regarding the size of black men's genitals and their sexual prowess became a potent symbol of the possible dishonor of white men through the sexual conquest of their women by black men. The power of this symbolic association is evident in the fact that black men did not need actually to touch a white women to be accused of rape and brutally punished. (This is one way to understand the killing of fifteen-year-old Emmett Till, who was savagely murdered in the South in the 1950s, ostensibly for leering at a white woman.) The inability of black women to retain their honor as women in this setting, and the inability of black men to defend their honor by protecting black women, resulted in the symbolic "masculinization" of black women and "feminization" of black men. (In a painful scene in Toni Morrison's novel *Beloved*, she tells the story of the sexual exploitation of black male slaves by their white captors.[27])

Third, the dynamics of honor and shame in American slavery were associated with racial purity. The shame of slavery was the lot of every person who could be proven to have one drop of African blood. It did not matter how much Caucasian blood a person had, it could not overcome the "stain of blackness." When the opportunity presented itself, some slaves chose to "pass" into the white world in order to escape the shame of blackness.

The system of honor and shame that existed in the South during slavery continues to affect the lives of African Americans. Although the language of honor and shame is rarely used, the deep-seated need for what the word "honor" represents is a permanent feature of life. Because black persons still live, in many ways, outside of the circles of influence that enclose their existence, the musical form of "the blues" has been the traditional mode of expressing the lament of shame. Evelyn Brooks Higginbotham describes the quest of black Baptist women at the beginning of the twentieth century for "respectability."[28] Later in the century Aretha Franklin still asks for "a little R E S P E C T."[29] The call for respect is the call for honor and more. It is a plea for a new system of social evaluation which honors everyone but does not depend on the degradation of anyone.

Honor and Shame in the Bible

The role of the Bible, and especially the New Testament, in the construction and deconstruction of the rhetoric of honor and shame is important for two basic reasons.[30] First, the New Testament as a text is itself part of the fabric of a Mediterranean society. The raw material for its fictive strategies and narrative praxis includes the structures of human evaluation that are intrinsic to that society. Second, the New Testament as a text often subverts the structures of human evaluation common to its social context, offering new ways to see human beings and human communities. These aspects of the New Testament suggest the need for a critical hermeneutical approach to scripture much like that developed in slave Christianity in the United States. That approach understood the message of scripture within the context of social struggle and highlighted those aspects of scripture that supported the liberation of human beings from inhumane social, political, economic, and religious forces.

Rereading key New Testament texts in light of the motifs of honor and shame might reveal some distinctive features of the African American hermeneutical tradition and further contribute to the continuing development of key themes in African American theology.

African American slaves in the southern United States found themselves living in a culture that shared with Mediterranean cultures a preoccupation with notions of honor and shame. African slave Christians, living in such a culture, were able to read the Bible in a way that noted its use and misuse of the themes of honor and shame. Their reading yielded a message that reversed normative social principles regarding honor and shame and allowed those enslaved to live as persons who, though shamed by the world, found honor in the eyes of God.

Two central portions of the New Testament reveal most clearly the reversal of these themes of honor and shame. They are the narratives about Jesus in Luke-Acts and Paul's Roman and Corinthian correspondence. While the theological assumptions undergirding the observations that follow can be described as liberation-oriented, they cannot be confined to the stereotypes that attend to certain liberation perspectives. In "liberation" perspectives Jesus is often seen as one who focused on *the social dimensions* of freedom. That is, Jesus is seen as the social radical who is at the same time the advocate of personal piety and conservatism. Within these same perspectives the Apostle Paul is often seen as one who focused on *the personal dimensions* of freedom. That is, Paul is the social conservative who is at the same time the advocate of a radical personal holiness. This is the root of those liberation Christologies that depict Jesus as the antagonist of the ruling religious and political order. It is also at the heart of the depiction of Paul as accommodationist with regard to the social-political environment, especially slavery in his letter to Philemon. A rereading of key texts, however, reveals a Jesus who provides a personal model for living in an honor and shame culture and a Paul who provides a social/communal example for living in such a culture.

Jesus, Honor, and Shame

Jesus' life and times were circumscribed by structures of human evaluation based on honor and shame. Although one cannot deny the fact that Jesus opposed the social and political structures of his day, his opposition might be better grasped by noting how in his life and ministry he subverted and even reversed existing notions of honor and shame on the personal level. In their work on honor and shame in Luke-Acts, Bruce J. Malina and Jerome H. Neyrey identify several features of Jesus' life and ministry that bear on this discussion.[31]

First, *although Jesus had no legitimate claim to male honor socially defined, he redefined male honor.* In Jesus' social context, according to Malina and Neyrey, "male honor is symbolized by the testicles, which stand for manliness, courage, authority over family, willingness to defend one's reputation, and refusal to submit to humiliation. . . . His masculinity, moreover, is in doubt if he maintains sexual purity and does not challenge the boundaries of others through their women."[32] Jesus refused to be defined as a man by his sexual conquests. Indeed, the long-held assumption regarding his celibacy suggests that traditional markers of maleness are superseded in his life. Moreover, Jesus was willing to submit to the humiliation of the cross, and to risk being viewed as a man who could not protect his mother when he entrusted her care to one of his disciples. He cared little for his reputation and was more likely to be found serving his family than exercising authority over them. There are numerous examples of this model of masculinity being partially fulfilled in African American Christian praxis. The Civil Rights Movement of the 1950s and 1960s drew much of its strength from the unusual sight of black men submitting to humiliation without retaliation. The Million Man March of 1995 brought together more than a million African American men to an occasion of atonement and recommitment to basic values. Notions of sexual conquests and familial authority as signs of manhood have been difficult for African American Christians to completely resist, however. Yet that is exactly what this picture of Jesus calls for.

Second, *in spite of the existing social codes regarding female shame, Jesus associated with shameless women.* With respect to women, shame carries a double meaning. Shame is positive, from the male perspective, in that "it refers to a woman's sensitivity about what others think, say, and do with regard to her worth . . . female shame (having shame), then is a positive value in a woman; a woman branded as 'shameless' means for a female what being shamed means for a male."[33] A woman is dishonorable when she has no shame or is *shameless*. This occurs when her chastity or sexual exclusiveness is lost (for example, prostitutes); when she is not under the dominion of a male (for example, widows and divorced women); or anytime she steps outside of socially defined boundaries or displays the assertiveness usually reserved for males. Not only did Jesus associate with these women deemed "shameless and dishonored"; he gave them a special place in the economy of salvation. Jesus' ministry to the woman with the issue of blood (Luke 8:43-48), the woman who washed Jesus feet with her tears (Luke 7:36-39), the persistent widow (Luke 18:1-8), and Mary when she insisted that her place was not just in the kitchen (Luke 10:38-42) are examples of his reversal of the social codes of honor and shame. African American women have endured the labels of shamelessness, sexual promiscuity, unfeminine assertiveness, and of being suited only to domestic labor. Within the stories of Jesus' dealing with shameless women are new models of human evaluation in which many black women have found redemptive significance.

Third, *although his social circumstances belie the fact, Jesus claimed honor by virtue of his bloodlines and his name.* In the social world of the New Testament "honor is always presumed to exist within one's family of blood, among all of one's blood relatives. A person can always trust blood relatives. Outside that circle, all people are presumed dishonorable . . . blood replicates honor; with blood relatives there is no honor contest."[34] Honor is also related to one's name. "To know the family name is to know the honor rating of an individual."[35] One's name functions as a social label indicating one's place in society. In the Lukan account of Jesus' birth, the low socioeconomic status of Mary and Joseph is countered by the claim that Jesus comes from royal bloodlines. He claims the honor bestowed on him by his kinsman John the Baptist. Although he is not granted honor by his townspeople of Nazareth during his initial appearance, because he is merely "the son of Joseph," the ascribed honor that accompanies the one called "the son of God" is his. African American Christians have historically drawn upon the parallels between Jesus' claim to honor and their own predicament. In spite of humble circumstances of birth, shifting kinship arrangements, and obscure or hidden bloodlines, African American Christians have found in the biblical text the basis for a positive self-evaluation. Although social circumstances contribute to such improvised kinship patterns as extended family structures, African American Christians claim the ascribed honor due to those who are brothers and sisters in Christ. This honor is claimed not only in relation to their kinship with Christ but by claiming a noble past. Those black Christians who are brothers and sisters in Christ are also the sons and daughters of Africa. Although their names often reflect their slave past, the fact that Jesus calls them "by name" grants an honor that is irrevocable by social circumstances.

Fourth, *although Jesus possesses no wealth he claims the acquired honor of a benefactor.* In addition to claims of noble birth, the major avenue to honor in the New Testament world was through the practice of patronage. The purpose of patronage was to fend off all challenges to one's honor by pointing to one's accomplishments in the public realm. "Acquired honor is the socially recognized claim to worth that a person obtains by achievements, such as benefactions (Luke 7:4-5) or prowess (Luke 7:16-17)." In Luke's world, honor is particularly acquired by excelling over others in the social interaction that we call challenge and riposte. "Challenge-riposte is a type of social interaction in which people hassle each other according to socially defined rules in order to gain the honor of another. . . . Challenge-riposte describes a constant social tug of war, a game of social push and shove."[36] This social game has three phases: (*a*) a challenge to one's honor is issued through word or deed, (*b*) this challenge is recognized as such by the receiver as well as the public at large, and (*c*) the challenge is rebuffed and the rebuttal is acknowledged as successful by the public. Jesus found himself constantly engaged in this social tug of war. Although the challenges issued to Jesus had religious import, it should not be overlooked that the social-rhetorical structures in which those challenges occurred were those of the honor and shame game. Jesus is challenged for healing on the Sabbath; he is challenged by the rich young ruler who saw his public accomplishments in keeping the law as warrant for the confirmation of his honor by Jesus. Jesus rebuffed these challenges by noting that grandiose public displays of beneficence were no guarantees that one would be honored in heaven. The widow's mite, faith the size of a mustard seed, the law kept within the human heart, and a prayer privately uttered, are all raised to the status of honorable benefactions. In essence, even the poorest person of faith could acquire honor in the kingdom of heaven.

African American Christians have historically not been in a social position to acquire honor through benefaction. Disposable wealth, until the latter part of the twentieth century, has been available to only a small minority of African Americans. Jesus' reversal of the normative claims to acquired honor, however, has shown that even small acts of hope, faith, and love are worthy of note. Perhaps the most striking example of this theme in African American letters is found in the autobiographical work of Booker T. Washington, *Up from Slavery*.[37] Writing from his experience as an ex-slave during the post-Reconstruction period, Washington was well aware of the honor-bound culture of the American South. He also knew that the primary source of honor in the antebellum South was one's noble birth. Therefore honor was symbolized by respectable bloodlines and shame by the lack of them. Although close analysis of Washington's text in light of the themes of honor and shame is outside the scope of this discussion, even a cursory reading reveals that Washington saw that the system of ascribed honor that characterized the antebellum South had been dismantled by the economic and social collapse following the Civil War. What Washington proposed in his philosophy was a new manifestation of honor and shame, focused on work and merit (two of Washington's favorite terms) as the sources of honor and on sloth and wastefulness as the sources of shame. Most analyses of Washington's philosophy focus on his desire to equip a people recently emancipated from slavery for the American industrial revolution. Yet an overlooked emphasis is the construction of a new system of human evaluation that would have a place for former slaves to acquire honor and avoid shame by performing meritorious service to society in the form of honest, if humble, labor.

Jesus' ministry within a culture of honor and shame was revolutionary in its presentation of a new system of human valuation. In the New Testament world honor was understood, as wealth sometimes is today, to exist in limited quantities. People were locked in a competitive battle for honor in which one could only become a winner by making someone else a loser. It was the currency of a system of social stratification and economic ordering that mandated an ongoing struggle for dominance and control. This observation sheds new light on Jesus' response to a situation in which his loyalty to the Roman empire was questioned: "Give to the emperor the things that are the emperor's, and to God the things that are God's" (Mark 12:17). "In a society in which religion and economics were embedded in politics, Jesus' answer clearly points to God as the only source of life, possessions, and honor."[38]

The Lukan picture of Jesus rejects oppressive notions of honor and shame and yields a new personal conception of grace. Grace is a fortuitous rupture in the iron competitive mechanism of the honor and shame game.

Paul, Honor, and Shame

Attention to the honor and shame culture of the New Testament world also yields fresh insights into the message of the Apostle Paul. Paul both adopts and adapts existing social codes in his attempts to describe and influence the character of the early Christian community. As Halvor Moxnes has observed, it is primarily through his writings in Romans that Paul attends to the two most important themes in relation to honor and shame.[39]

First, Paul argues that the Christian community, although ensconced within a Mediterranean culture of the first century, in certain important respects should be a distinct human gathering. His primary concern is the upbuilding of the Christian community. Within the context of an honor and shame culture, the Christian community should be organized according to different principles. Paul's concern in Romans was to bring together in one community both Jews and Gentiles. This task was complicated by the fact that the Jews traditionally employed a vocabulary of privilege when it came to their status as the heirs of the promise. That is, the Jewish Christians at Rome claimed a place of honor for themselves that was not granted to the Gentiles. Paul took this vocabulary and used it to express the identity of the entire Christian community. In doing so he radically changed that vocabulary to reflect the new values that undergirded the existence of the new community in Christ. As Halvor Moxnes observes:

> Paul is concerned how the *Christians, both Jewish and non-Jewish,* can find their own identity. In his mission Paul broke down the barriers between Jews and non-Jews. This was a source of conflict with the synagogues, and thus the Pauline communities needed to find a separate identity vis-à-vis the synagogue. At the same time the emerging groups needed to find a way to function within Graeco-Roman society. Within the context of this search for a new identity the issue of honour and shame played an important role in relation to Graeco-Roman society and to the synagogue was well as within the Christian groups themselves.[40]

This new community, as described in Romans 13, is not utopian in the sense that its members are unaware of or inattentive to their social context or their civic obligations. "In the public sphere Christians found themselves in a stratified society with rulers and subordinates united by a common quest for honour and praise. Paul makes a strong case that Christians should accept the obligations of their society."[41] In Romans 1 and 6, however, Paul urges a reassessment of the outside world and its stratifications. Here "Paul's concern is with humanity in relation to God. Therefore honour is not a civic virtue but is exclusively reserved for God; it is his glory (*doxa,* 1.21, 23) and his power (1.20). And it is humanity's duty to render the honour which is due to God (1.21)."[42] In this instance, the focus is not on worldly honor and shame. Shame takes on a new significance. "Shame is the mark of the life of non-believers and of the former life of Christians. . . . In Romans 6 the opposite of 'shame' is not 'honour' but 'holiness' (*hagiasmos,* 6.19, 22), a word which indicates distinction and separateness from society at large. Thus, the description of the outside world as shameful functions as a border against the non-Christian world in which the Christians are a separate group of holy people."[43]

The most significant aspect of the early Christian community was Paul's emphasis on an equality (not uniformity) within its internal life, which called into question and challenged the honor and shame culture in which it was situated. This equality (or inclusiveness) meant that those who were accustomed to privilege had to accommodate themselves to different roles in the Christian community. Paul introduced "an ideal of equality with respect to honour which must have created tensions within the community. Individuals who had status and resources were asked to undertake functions of leadership, but were denied that recognition and honour which was supposed to accompany such behavior. Paul emphasized unity so much that he asked benefactors and leaders to forgo their just recognition."[44] They were denied *honor* but were accorded *respect* (Romans 2:7; 2:10; 12:10; 13:7; and 1 Corinthians 12:23).

This distinction between Paul's references to the Christian community as a community in the world and a community apart from the world can help to explain the passages where the Apostle Paul is sometimes thought to be inconsistent in his proclamation. Paul uses the language of honor and shame in ways that can be best described as paradoxical in Romans 1 and 8. Christians find heavenly honor or holiness in God's estimation in spite of wearing the label of terrestrial shame, and divine power in spite of worldly weakness. "Power in weakness, confidence of honour while seemingly put to shame—that was the paradox of Christian existence in a Jewish and Graeco-Roman environment."[45] For the early Christians their status as heirs was not visible to the outside world. Nor was it within the power of the outside world to revoke. As a community founded on new social principles, yet existing within the context of ancient ones, the early church was to be the embodiment of a new structure of human evaluation. In essence, the early church was to be the embodiment of grace.

It is toward *grace* that the Apostle Paul urges the fledgling churches. It is within the context of an honor and shame society that his notion of grace is shaped. Three moments in Paul's journey toward grace are especially important for this discussion. The first is the apostle's preaching regarding *shame* and *boasting*. He understood fully the social meaning of shame in his time, and within this understanding he asserted, "I am not ashamed of the Gospel" (Romans 1:16). Certainly he was not referring to the contemporary meaning of shame. Shame pointed to a paradox in the experience of Christians. Shame properly described the social estimation of early Christians. They were, almost by definition, dishonorable. But from the perspective of faith, they were not ashamed of foolishness of belief or the folly of Christian preaching. The other side of this paradox is the Apostle's preaching regarding *boasting*. Outside of the Christian community, Paul defends his right to boast, to claim an honor that is apparently not his to claim. In 2 Corinthians 10 and 11 Paul defends his ministry and argues for its legitimacy using the more effective rhetorical devices of the day.[46] He makes it clear that through through his heritage as an Israelite he has inherited the right to boast and through his sufferings he has paid the price to justify his boasting. Unlike that of the world, Paul's boasting "has proper limits" and is confined to the field that God has defined. Within the Christian community, Paul warns against boasting because it exposes the community to the deleterious patterns of human evaluation regnant in the outside world. In Romans 3:27 and 4:2 he links boasting within the community with false claims to honor. These false claims are associated with the observance of the Law as a means to salvation and thus, honor. By reminding the early Christians that no one could rightly boast of having achieved salvation through observance of the Law, Paul sought to remove the major impediment to solidarity within the community.

It is within this paradox of shame and boasting in the Christian community that Paul's message of grace is to be understood. This is the second moment in Paul's journey to grace. "Honor" within the community cannot be obtained through the usual means. In Romans Paul argues that neither the merit of good works (4:2-4), nor the strict observance of the Law (3:27-28), nor being circumcised will bring the appropriate honor to the faithful. This "honor" or "righteousness" is awarded as a free gift (4:4-5). It is the fact that this righteousness is given as a free gift that makes it a gracious act of God toward humanity. This segment of the Pauline message is a familiar one because it articulates the notion of justification by faith rather than by works. Looking at the framing of this argument within an honor and shame perspective, however, casts new light on a passage within the Pauline corpus which some interpreters have found problematic.

> To those who by persistence in doing good seek glory, honor and immortality, he will give eternal life. But for those who are self-seeking and who reject the truth and follow evil, there will be wrath and anger. There will be trouble and distress for every human being who does evil: first for the Jew, then for the Gentile; but glory, honor and peace for everyone who does good: first for the Jew, then for the Gentile. For God does not show favoritism.
>
> (Rom. 2:7-11; New International Version)

This passage appears to argue against the notion of justification by faith alone. As one interpreter has argued, however, Paul, working within an honor and shame context, is not addressing the theological question of justification by faith. He is making the point "that there is no distinction between Jews and non-Jews: both groups will receive honour or pun-ishment on the same basis, that is, on the basis of good or evil acts."[47]

The third moment in Paul's journey involves an understanding of how God's grace allows the Christian community to live *in* the world but not be *of* the world. This understanding suggests that the Christian community did not and could not live and function completely inde-pendently of its social context. Christian values of charity and humility were not simply set over and against the external values of honor and shame. Instead, through Christian preaching and teaching, honor and shame were given new meaning and content. It is especially through the preaching of Paul that a new pattern of honor and human worth are articulated. In his preaching, "what eventually becomes clear is that it is not [Paul's] honor at all which is at stake, but the presuppositions of the community "regarding what is honorable and what is shame-ful."[48] Seeing humanity from an eschatological perspective, Paul could establish a utopian vision of honor that rescued Christians from grace-lessness. It is through living out this eschatological reality that the Christian community finds the means of grace.

Many traditional African American churches are organized in ways that are curious to outsiders. Within these churches is a basic paradox of freedom and form. On the one hand, these churches exhibit a free, and sometimes spontaneous worship style, accompanied by music that freely searches the aesthetic horizon to find the key to the meaning of black Christian experience. This freedom is embodied within the black church itself and is a reflection of the fact that God's grace is a free gift. The iron grip of competition is loosed within this community as they celebrate the free abundance of God's love. On the other hand, these churches also exhibit a formality in terms of the choreography of worship and commu-nity life. Ushers function according to a strict pattern of practice. The same is true of the functions of deacons, trustees, and the nurses' guild. The chaos of oppression and despair is contained within the formal recognition of God's love. Paul Tillich once observed that the Christian community exists along the continuum of form and dynamism. Through grace African American Christians have sought that balance between a sterile formality and formless energy. When they are successful a collection of *worldly weaklings* can become a *divine powerhouse*.

From Honor to Amazing Grace

In the 1960s a group of anthropologists gathered and defined a field of study related to honor and shame in Mediterranean cultures. In the late 1980s a group that included some of the earlier writers gathered to look again at the notion of honor but concluded that one could not adequately understand the function of honor within a given culture without attention to the idea of *grace*.[49] The resulting volume on grace in anthropology takes into account the massive Christian theological literature on grace that has been produced but also addresses dimensions of grace that most anthropologists and even theologians neglect or overlook. Julian Pitt-Rivers observes that "No anthropologist has to my knowledge asked himself whether there is anything remotely equivalent to grace among the concepts of Buddhism, Hinduism, Shintoism, or Taoism . . . [or] whether the problem to which the doctrines of grace tender an answer has no echo beyond the religions of the Book, let alone the peoples without writing, or whether grace can be treated as a universal concept or only as an element of Western culture."[50] Like honor, the meaning of grace is fluid and responds to its context. Grace can refer to the words said before the consumption of a meal or to a personal characteristic of graciousness or gracefulness or, as a gratuity, to an additional payment left for good service at a restaurant. While honor always refers to some social obligation, grace always refers in one way or another to a free gift. Either grace is the precondition which makes the acceptance of that gift possible (prevenient grace), or it is the active response to the gift that is freely given (the Thomistic or scholastic definition of grace). A common sense of gratuity defines the term "grace." Grace, then, allows no payment, demands no explanation, and requires no justification:

> It is not just illogical, but opposed to logic, a counter-principle, unpredictable as the hand of God, an "unfathomable mystery" which stretches far beyond the confines of theology. The opposition is clear and applies in every case: grace is opposed to calculation, as chance is to the control of destiny, as the free gift is to the contract, as the heart is to the head, as the total commitment is to the limited responsibility, as thanks are to the stipulated counterpart, as the notion of community is to that of alterity, as *Gemeinschaft* is to *Gesellschaft*, as kinship amity is to political alliance, as the open cheque is to the audited account.[51]

While there is a tendency to associate the qualities of grace with women, and those of honor with men, these studies of honor and grace support the conclusion that grace of God is the foundation of all true honor.

Within African American Christianity the idea of grace is fundamental to human evaluation. Grace conforms itself to the suffering and shame of the downtrodden, and grace transforms the quality of life itself, imputing honor in the midst of disgrace. Traditionally the doctrine of grace has been one of the most complex themes within European and American theology. It has occupied the attention of theologians from Tertullian to Aquinas and from Augustine to Karl Barth to Karl Rahner. Yet surprisingly little has been written on the doctrine of grace in African American theology. It is my argument that the African American quest for a positive evaluation in the sight of God and in the eyes of other human beings can be a fruitful starting point for an African American doctrine of grace.

Three themes need attention and explication in the formulation of an African American doctrine of grace. These themes are drawn from the ways in which grace actually functions in African American Christian experience. First, *grace addresses the condition of those who are lost.* We have noted that those persons who suffer shame in a culture based on honor and shame often employ the rhetoric of loss to express the condition of dishonor. In African American Christianity, the experience of loss becomes the plight of the lost. This is one of the reasons that the hymn "Amazing Grace" is so popular in African American churches. While this hymn is certainly sung by other racial and ethnic Christians, within African American experience, the words, "I once was lost, but now I'm found," form the backdrop for the meaning of grace. The concept of *perdition* in traditional European-American theology is related to this experience of being lost. Augustine, for example, consistently refers to humanity as one single mass of sin. The term that he uses to describe this condition is *massa perditionis* or "mass of perdition." The word "perdition" refers to the state of being lost. Because all of humanity is lost in sin, no honor that befalls a person is in any way a commendation of his or her worthiness. If anything, this gratuitous honor or grace is the evidence of divine freedom and election. The problem with Augustine's notion of perdition is that it relates primarily to the bondage of the will and the shackles that accompany our natural being. Much of Western theology has been concerned with the psychological liberation of the Christian consciousness from the natural realm and with separating the gracious acts of God from human nature. In African American experience grace is understood as escape, not from the bondage of the will, but from the enslavement of the person:

> *Through many dangers, toils and snares,*
> *I have already come.*
> *It was grace that brought us safe thus far*
> *and grace will lead us home.*

41

Grace does not mandate the simple rejection of human nature, but is God's way of redeeming human nature in unexpected ways:

> *Amazing grace will always be my song of praise.*
> *It was grace which bought my liberty.*
> *I don't know why he came to love me so.*
> *He looked beyond my fault and saw my need.*[52]

Grace is the means by which God saves persons lost in the quagmire of sin, shame, and disgrace.

Second, *grace does not debilitate human effort, but supports and undergirds it, rooting it in thanksgiving.* In one school of traditional theology grace has been understood as the power of God that has been "infused" into humanity and enables the exercise of the human will. Grace understood in this way does not set the freedom of God over against the freedom of the human will. It thereby avoids the pitfalls of the inevitable problem of predestination. It is an understanding of grace which supports the human capacity to shape the future. Yet the problem with this view of grace is that it is often associated with *individualism* and the idea of *meritocracy.* Sin is viewed as the transgression of individuals against the divine/human compact. Thus, grace is understood as the redemption of the individual. In this sense, grace is something that can be merited or earned. This is the scholastic view of grace. In African American Christianity, both sin and grace are understood as social phenomena. Sin is not merely the violation of divine mandates by individuals, nor is grace only the salvation of the individual. Grace is rooted in gratitude. This gratitude does not mean that all human effort is rendered meaningless. It means that human effort finds its ultimate justification in a place much deeper than a competitive game of oneupsmanship. Grace lifts the group, grace is social: grace is communal. The depth of grace is apparent in the frequency with which the words, "Thank you, Jesus" are uttered in the context of African American Christian worship.

Third, *grace does not depend on human effort but takes it beyond its natural limits toward abundance.* In another traditional view of grace, it comes to humanity as a gift separate from and independent of any human effort. In this view God's grace cannot be thwarted by human recalcitrance, nor is human assistance necessary. Grace is irresistible, and once given, a permanent possession. In this sense the human will is subordinate to the divine will. This view of grace emphasizes that God is sovereign. The problem with this view of grace is that it is often associated with a skewed concept of *election* and the idea of *divine right*. Sin is viewed as a rebellion against grace, an "impossible" desire to live outside of a relationship with God. In this sense, grace is a "given" in Christian life. It is a gift. This is the reformed view of grace. In African American Christian experience neither sin nor grace can be understood apart from who we are as beings created by God. That is, sin does attend to our "nature" as finite human beings, because we can and do misuse our freedom. While the reach of God's grace is not confined to what is possible within our nature as human beings, that grace is not unnatural. In African American experience grace is rooted in abundance. Grace makes us more than we are: grace means that we are chosen by God and that our chosenness does not mean that others are not chosen. Grace does not allow us to limit it or to withhold it from others. It is a gift. It is abundance. It is superfluence. The horizon of grace is seen in the frequency with which the words "Have mercy, Lord" are uttered in African American Christian worship.

A fresh understanding of grace can assist African American Christians in particular, and Christians in general, in addressing some of the more complex ethical and theological issues of our time. A new view of grace can liberate us from the iron competition that so often characterizes an honor and shame culture. Grace can transform our rhetoric of loss into words of thanksgiving. Grace can bring esteem to a people who are continually disrespected. In the words of an anonymous black Christian saint, grace happens "somewhere between 'Have mercy, Lord' and 'Thank you, Jesus.'"

Health, Disease, and Salvation

But I will restore you to health and heal your wounds, because you are called an outcast, Zion for whom no one cares.
——Jeremiah 30:17

For many people in the African American community, life in the contemporary world should carry a warning similar to that found on tobacco products: *It can be hazardous to your health.* Threats to the health of African Americans are deeply rooted in the social structures of Western culture. Those threats are more obviously manifested in the ubiquity of advertising for tobacco products and alcoholic beverages in many African American communities, although the problem is more deeply rooted than the images of Joe Camel selling cigarettes or a bull selling malt liquor. The healing and wholeness of black people is obstructed by powerful forces in American society that are difficult to isolate and even more difficult to resist. The tremendous growth in medical technology, scientific advances in treatments, as well as new discoveries in various medical fields, have further complicated the issue of what it means to be healthy in our culture. Yet for African Americans the issue of their physical health is inseparable from the ravages of racism upon their humanity. There is a deep suspicion of the medical delivery system among many black people in the United States. This suspicion is rooted in the collective memory of incidents like the infamous Tuskegee Experiment. Beginning in the 1930s, more than four hundred black men were either purposely infected with syphilis or simply diagnosed and left untreated. The disease was allowed to progress in these men even though effective treatments were readily available. The sole purpose of this experiment was to chart the progress of the disease until the subjects died. This experiment was conducted within the boundaries of the law and was halted in 1972 as a result of public outcry. The horror of the medical establishment's willingness to sacrifice the health and lives of these black men for the sake of advancing medical science, is exceeded only by the insult of being consistently denied access to the medical delivery systems. The historical experience of being denied access to "white only" hospitals during legal segregation has been overlaid with the contemporary experience of being denied quality health care. The nightmare of the Tuskegee Experiment is the backdrop for the persistent rumors that AIDS is the result of a genocidal plot in which the virus was artificially developed and intentionally introduced into the black population in Africa, the Caribbean, and the United States. It is less important to note that irrefutable substantiation of this rumor would be difficult to produce than it is to see that African Americans often feel vulnerable and live in an environment of fear and trepidation. This in and of itself is not healthy.

One of the tasks of ministry is to advance the spiritual health of the Christian community. Ministers are called to be "physicians of the soul." For people of African descent, however, one cannot separate the health of the soul from that of the whole person. The health of the whole person may include, but is not the same as, the full functioning of all the biological systems in the physical body. We are more than flesh and bone; we are our bodies and more. There are other religious and even Christian groups that harbor their own suspicion of and ambivalence toward modern Western medicine (for example, Christian Scientists). Yet the health problems of black folk are deeply rooted in their exclusion from and marginalization within Western culture and societies.

This chapter addresses the problem of health in African American experience as a theological problem. By exposing the religious underpinnings of this issue, we might uncover insights that will enhance the work of those who minister to and with African American people. The basic assumption is that this is not a problem of medical ethics but something much more fundamental. The question of who receives quality medical care in our society is, at heart, a question of who shall be saved. The theological issue here is soteriology or our understanding of salvation. The language of soteriology is almost never used in discussing this issue because that language is associated with the narrow theological discussions of sin. When the concept of health is discussed, it is most often juxtaposed with the concept of illness. My thesis, however, is that the concept of health, when referring to black people, is discussed in muted tones and within the narrative framework of a *rhetoric of disease*.

We begin with a brief examination of the most animated public discussion of health in recent years; the debate on the Health Security Act proposed in the early 1990s. The truncated character of this debate suggests that deeper issues remain unaddressed. A conceptual overview of the major scholarly discussions of *disease* in the field of medical anthropology will then provide the context for a brief examination of this concept in the experience of black people in Western cultural systems. It will be important to note how the Bible speaks to the notions of health and disease before concluding with a proposal for revising our theological understanding of salvation.

The Health Care Debate: More than a Question of Ethics

In the early 1990s the debate over health care in the United States was initiated by the realization that many of the nation's social problems were actually health problems. Tens of millions of people lacked either the resources to obtain quality medical care or the insurance coverage to guarantee access. While a significant portion (14 percent) of the national gross product was spent annually on health care, a large percentage of the population found such care beyond their reach. The response to this problem was the introduction of the 1993 Health Security Plan by the President of the United States. The aim of this plan was to guarantee that every American citizen had access to quality medical care. For our purposes, the details of the plan and its relative merits or faults are less important than the way in which the issues were rhetorically framed. The introduction of the notion of universal coverage spawned four major questions, but in the final analysis those questions left unaddressed the fundamental issue. First, the idea of universal health care presented a *political/economic* question: How can we provide universal access to quality health care, and at the same time control spiraling costs? Here the issue is one of determining the principles, in terms of money and power, by which this commodity called health care is allocated. Second, it presented an *ethical* question: Is not health care a fundamental good to which each American citizen is entitled?[1] Or is it the case, as former Surgeon General C. Everett Koop put it, that "What's good for each American is not necessarily good for all Americans and what's good for all Americans is not necessarily good for each American?"[2] Here the issue is one of determining whether health care is a fundamental good or a relative good; whether it is primarily an individual possession or a community possession. At this point the public conversation reached its most heated and unproductive stage. It simply pitted individual rights over group responsibilities; and given the propensity toward individualism in U.S. society, the conversation was largely doomed to futility. Third, the debate on health care in the United States presented a *cultural* question: Is not the issue of universal entitlement to health care shaped by a Darwinian bias toward the survival of the fittest amidst the inexorable forces of the marketplace?[3] The issue here is whether the idea of universal health care coverage is antithetical to our closely held notions of what it means to be an American. The fourth question emerging out of the debate was a *moral* one. Quentin D. Young, a physician, offered these reflections on the formation of that moral question in his experience at Cook County Hospital in Chicago:

> Whatever there was, County had. And you see the most disenfranchised, the most impoverished, the wretched of the earth. I was just a middle-class, kind of liberal person, but it became clear that a doctor at County could adopt one of two philosophies—and the staff was about evenly divided along these lines. About half the doctors felt that they were witnessing divine justice, a heavenly—or Darwinian—retribution for evil ways, for excesses in drugs, in booze and everything else. Patients came to the hospital with their breath laden with alcohol, with needle marks on their arms, their babies illegitimate and all the rest. The other half decided that here was the congealed oppression of our society—people whose skin color, economic position, place of birth, family size, you name it—operated to give them a very short stick. When you saw them medically and psychologically in that broken, oppressed state, it was clear that you had to address issues of justice, not just medical treatment. I had to decide which of these value systems was fair and just, and which one I could live with. It seemed to me the first approach is judgmental and harsh and simplistic. Taking the alternative view gave me a shot at being a part of the human race.[4]

Although the cultural and moral questions had the potential to open public discourse to the deeper theological questions involved, that potential was unrealized because of the absence of significant theological analysis and because the underlying question centered on who would take care of the poor. The ethical debate on health care stalled because the problem was subtly recast as a problem of *the poor*. Since the end of the mass immigration of persons from Europe early in the twentieth century, the poor has become a way of referring to those persons who are marginal to society. While various ethnic groups have and will continue to move in and out of this category, this term, the poor, has always been, in many important ways, synonymous with black people. As Toni Morrison notes in her brilliant essay, *Playing in the Dark*, black people have historically been a *cipher* in our national discourse.[5] It is my contention that within the deep narrative structures and beneath the broad cultural connotations of health in our society, lies a *rhetoric of disease*. Unless this rhetoric is critically examined, it will be difficult, if not impossible, to understand the meaning of health in our times and why human wholeness has proven to be such an elusive virtue for the Christian community.

A Conceptual Overview of Health and Disease

Concern with health and disease has always been a part of human experience.[6] In every age and culture, a singular and universal threat to life and well-being has come from those conditions we call "disease." Disease is as old as life itself "because disease is nothing else but life, life under changed circumstances."[7] It is precisely the different ways in which the forces that control those circumstances of human life are construed that results in the major medical theories and their concomitant views of health and disease.

Literature on health and disease is substantial, and a full exposition of the topic would take us far beyond the scope of this chapter. But several major thematic emphases, present in that literature, will contribute to an understanding of the rhetorical function of the concept of disease in Western culture.

Among the oldest understandings of health and disease is that of ancient Egypt. The Egyptians developed a sophisticated understanding of human biological systems. This knowledge enabled them to develop the embalming processes for which they are still famous. Beyond their knowledge of the human anatomy itself, they understood something of the biochemical processes by which matter decomposed. They employed their knowledge to delay or virtually halt the process of decomposition, which they referred to as *putrefaction*. This notion of putrefaction was the basis of their understanding of health and disease. Disease occurred when nutriments were taken into the body but not absorbed. These nutriments remained in the organs, were warmed by the natural heat of the body, and underwent putrefaction, which result-ed in disease.[8] The Egyptian notion of health is the reverse of disease. Health is restored and maintained by ridding the body of these residues, which was the aim of medical practice in ancient Egypt. Despite the claims of some scholars, ancient Egyptian medicine had a rational basis, and many of its fundamental ideas were the legacy of ancient Egypt to Greece.[9]

The most influential theory of health and disease in Western culture is derived from the ancient Greeks. As far back as the time of Homer, the Greeks were concerned about physical health. For them, illness was a sign of the presence of evil. Homeric medicine made a distinction between what we would refer to as *disease* and illness. Illness basically referred to those external threats to health that persons encountered on the battlefield. To be ill was essentially to be *wounded*. This is why the *Iliad* and other Homeric poems so vividly recount the horrors of war. On the other hand, *disease* was internal and inflicted by the gods. Zeus, Apollo, or Artemis could show his displeasure by sending infir-mity to plague their human subjects.[10] Homeric physicians refused to treat persons with diseases, limiting their practice to those wounded in battle.

Following the Homeric period Greek notions of health and disease fell into two fairly distinct traditions. The first and dominant tradition was part of the philosophical schools that emerged in ancient Greece. In this tradition health is defined as the state of balance or equilibrium within the body; that is, those substances which make up the body must be maintained in specific proportions and in specific relationship to each other. Disease occurred when this balance or equilibrium was upset. Both Plato and Aristotle discussed health and disease in their attempts to describe the nature of human and cosmic reality. Pythago-ras, the mathematician, related health and disease to his view of reality. For him, as all of reality could be explained in numerical terms and existed in an ideal mathematical harmony, so "harmony, perfect equi-librium, perfect balance, were the goal of the Pythagorean life and also the key to health."[11] Disease occurred when that delicate balance was upset, and the cure was to restore that balance through diet, and, sur-prisingly, music. Of course, this view of health as balance and disease as imbalance was also characteristic of other ancient cultures, for example, the pre-Columbian societies of the Maya. Like many other philosophical ideas, their presence in Greek thought does not necessarily prove their origin in Greek thought.

The dominant figure in Greek medical thought was Hippocrates. Although some scholars have argued that he never really existed, it is generally believed that he was born about 460 B.C.E. on the island of Cos and died about 370 in Thessaly.[12] Hippocrates is credited with bringing the power of rationality to the practice of medicine. Hippocrates is best known for the body of writing which bears his name, the Hippocratic Collection. The *Corpus Hippocraticum* is a massive work that sets forth systematically a significant portion of the extant medical knowledge of the day. Although it is not likely that Hippocrates wrote the entire corpus, its main ideas are attributed to him. The major topics are anatomy, physiology, general pathology, therapy, diagnosis, prognosis, surgery, gynecology, obstetrics, mental illness, and ethics. In these treatises, the foundations of modern Western medicine were laid. Hippocrates' name is also associated with the Hippocratic Oath:

> In summary, this famous testament contains both affirmations and prohibitions. It begins with pledges to the gods and to teachers as well as future students. The prohibitions are against harm to the patient, deadly drugs, abortion, surgery, sexual congress with the patient or his household, and revelation of secrets discovered while ministering to the sick. The duties are to act with purity and holiness. The Oath is the most widely known document associated with the name of Hippocrates. Graduating medical students for centuries have stood to swear to its provisions (either unaltered or with modifications). Yet it is probably not a part of the Hippocratic teachings, was not in all likelihood sworn by physicians on Cos, and is at variance with some of the principles and practices of Hippocrates.[13]

Hippocrates is also known for the method that bears his name. the Hippocratic method refers to the unrelenting rationalism of Greek medical thought. This tradition eschewed religious and magical explanations for illness and disease. This method was built on four major principles: observe all, study the patient rather than the disease, evaluate honestly, and assist nature. With Hippocrates the physician is the scientist, medicine is the mastery of nature, and health and disease are no longer matters of mystery.

The second and subordinate tradition in Greek medical thought deals more specifically with the persistent notion that disease was connected with the wrath of the gods. When the Homeric physicians would not treat persons with internal diseases, sufferers went to various cultic priests who promised to help them placate the offended deities. Even during and after the time of Hippocrates, persons sought alternative causal explanations of health and disease. This religious system of medical thought centered around the mythical figure of Asclepios, the Greek god of healing. Numerous elaborate temples and a sophisticated system of medical treatment evolved from the adoration of Asclepios, beginning about the sixth century B.C.E. This medical system existed side by side with the practice of secular medicine in Greece, and the temples functioned as hospitals. Since the cause of disease in religious medical thought was the wrath of the gods, health could be restored only by appealing to the god of healing. In Asclepian temples patients underwent a series of treatments, including dietary prescriptions and ritual bathing. The most important component of the healing, however, called *incubation,* involved creating an atmosphere in which the patient fell into a sleeplike state. During the night the patient would be visited by a priest dressed as the god Asclepios. The priest, along with the temple assistants, would administer treatments that included traditional and secular methods. In this system the cure took place in the patient's dreams. In one important text in the field of medical history the following observation is offered:

> Clearly the most important ingredient in the effectiveness of the temple cure was faith. The suppliant's belief in the efficacy of the god was aided by accounts of cures on tablets and probably by oral descriptions given by temple assistants. . . . The religious and spiritual atmosphere was inspiring, and the appearance and ministrations of the priest acting as Asclepias, with his accompanying retinue, were doubtless impressive.[14]

The persistence of religious medicine in ancient Greece was due to some of the dramatic cures accomplished there, along with the refusal of secular physicians to treat what they thought were hopeless cases. For these patients there was nowhere else to turn for the restoration of the balance that constituted true health.

While Greek ideas of medical practice set the course of Western thought, four other major notions of health and disease were articulated in subsequent centuries. In the *naturalistic* view, health is defined as an appropriate lifespan that ends in natural death. Disease is the interruption of this natural process. The tragedy of disease is not that it might result in death but that it interrupts the natural processes of life. Philosophically speaking, disease is a permanent historical phenomenon that accompanies the historical existence of humanity. Disease takes a natural and historical course over time, just as human experience does. In this sense, the history of disease is part of human history. Disease is also a sign that nature has been violated. This view is most clearly articulated by the French philosopher Jean-Jacques Rousseau. According to Rousseau humanity enjoyed perfect health in its primitive, paradisiacal state. Disease was the result of civilization. It was not merely the changed environment which brought about disease, he believed, but the fact that, in civilization, humanity strove for more than it needed for life. This journey from a natural state to the attempted mastery of the universe has resulted in pain and disease.[15] In the *religious* view, as we have already noted, disease is associated with divine punishment, sin, and impurity. In the *moral* view, the source of disease is the inner struggle of humanity to control primitive impulses and desires. In Freudian terms, as human beings seek to curb aggression, unfulfilled desires often result in an assortment of maladies. Here disease is the result of sin, redefined as transgression against internal moral laws rather than against the external rule of the gods or against the laws of nature. In the *social* view, the roots of disease are found in the living conditions of modern industrial life. Health is restored by the provision of adequate sanitation, innoculation, and education. In this case, diseases are social "not because of the social nature of their causes, but because of their social implications."[16]

The Greek system of medicine has continued to define Western medicine at the level of rational thought and scientific practice. Other medical systems have emerged, all with their distinctive economies of health and disease, such as homeopathy, hydrotherapy, phrenology, osteopathy, chiropractic, and Christian Science. Some of these systems have stood over and against the dominant medical paradigm, while others have almost merged with it. Discussions of the philosophical connotations of health and disease have lost their centrality in medical thought with the emergence of *germ theory* and the discovery of the role of bacteria in the causal explanation of sickness. Yet notions of health and disease continue to function in our culture as rhetorical markers that help us to define our reality and to make sense of what we do not fully understand.

Several important moments in the development of the rhetoric of disease in Western culture merit brief mention here. First, is the discovery by Rudolph Virchow (1821–1902), a pioneer in the field of pathology in European medicine, that what we call disease is not one thing but a series of symptoms for which we have no other explanation. Disease is not caused by outside agents acting on the body; it is the result of the response or lack thereof by the body to internal or external changes. Disease, in the view of Virchow, "is but a figurative, imaginative and abstract unity. . . . it remains *an abstraction or pure thought, stimulated, however, by the concrete reality of observable phenomena and, above all, not denied by them.*"[17] With this insight the difference between health and disease is blurred, and the criteria for distinguishing between them become quite relative. Therefore "disease" becomes a label, a rhetorical convention, rather than a solution to a problem. H. Tristam Engelhardt Jr., notes that "Disease language is complex. . . . Further, disease language is performative; it creates social reality."[18] This purely formal definition of disease makes it possible to fill the category with a variety of content. For example, disease can take on a primarily social meaning. This has been true of syphilis throughout the centuries. As a disease it has no timeless meaning.[19] It has been a symbol for the defilement of Europe by so called pagan cultures, and it has been the symbol for the defilement of non-Western cultures by Europeans. Further, the development of the notion of disease as rhetorical category made it possible to use "disease" to refer to whatever we do not understand or by which we feel threatened, for example, people of other races. On the one hand, racial difference was sometimes admired because certain racial groups seemed resistant to certain diseases. This romantic view was applied to European Jews in the early nineteenth century.[20] More often, however, the rhetorical category of disease made it possible to identify certain racial groups as threats to public health. In the 1930s German National Socialist propaganda associated Jews with the Black Plague. Some medical historians linked Africa with leprosy. Disease became a convenient conceptual category within which to couch a purely irrational racism. The construction of a rhetoric of disease was enhanced by a debate on the nature of contagion. Humankind has always recognized that disease can be spread from person to person. This fact, however, has often been overshadowed by the belief that there were divine or cosmic reasons for its spread. In the eighteenth century in the United States and Europe a battle emerged between those persons who believed that disease was contagious and those who believed that disease was caused by environmental changes or internal bodily changes. The contagionists emerged victorious in this struggle, thereby enforcing the principles of quarantine. Disease as rhetorical device proved quite effective in buttressing arguments for racial segregation, isolation, and finally racial genocide or *ethnic cleansing.* This rhetoric has had a significant impact on the experience of African Americans and has been especially potent when linked with religious discourse.

Health and Disease in African American Experience

One way to understand the complexities of African American experience is to examine how the rhetoric of health and disease has been employed in setting limits and conscribing their life-chances. That rhetoric has taken a shape peculiar to the culture of the United States. Its roots, however, like those of many other ideological forces in the nation, lie in Europe. Within European culture the rhetoric of disease developed with distinct racial overtones. One of the more celebrated examples of this was the pornographic fascination of the European medical-scientific community with the physiognomy of Sarah Bartmann. She was a woman of the Hottentot tribe in South Africa who was exhibited as the "Hottentot Venus" throughout Europe for more than twenty-five years. Large European audiences gathered to view her naked body, which was of such scientific interest because of the size of her buttocks and her sexual organs. Even after her premature death in Paris in 1815, the fascination with her body continued as her private parts were preserved for viewing and study. Her black body was sacrificed in the interest of others. This account is important because the obviously sexual fascination of her captors was camouflaged by the rhetoric of disease. That is, it was argued that her body and the difference that she displayed were the result of disease. Therefore the study of her body was critical to the health of the general public. Black women and black sexuality were related to disease.[21]

The rhetoric of disease was a critical factor in the maintenance of American slavery. Although the argument that Africans were diseased was not the primary reason given for their enslavement, it was instrumental in the maintenance of the system of chattel slavery. One writer notes that "there is a long history of perceiving this [black] skin color as the result of some pathology. The favorite theory, which reappears with some frequency in the early nineteenth century, is that the skin color and physiognomy of the black are the result of congenital leprosy."[22] One of the major architects of the rhetoric of disease was Benjamin Rush:

> He was a founder of the Pennsylvania Society for Promoting the Abolition of Slavery, a member of the Continental Congress, a signer of the Declaration of Independence, an influential educator, and a philosopher of republican ideology. Moreover, he was a doctor of medicine, surgeon-general in the Revolutionary army, professor of the theory and practice of medicine at the University of Pennsylvania, and the head of the Pennsylvania Hospital's ward for the insane. Author of seminal books on the

diseases of the mind, he would later be regarded as the Father of American Psychiatry.[23]

Rush's view of the new republic was that its perfection could be attained through the practice of medicine. The greatest threat to public health, in Rush's view, is the presence of black people. In scholarly papers Rush argued that the black skin of African Americans was the result of a form of leprosy. Other marks of this diseased state were the size and shape of their lips, nose, and the texture of their hair. Interestingly, Rush argues that this disease does not impair the physical health of black people because it was not infectious within the race. Yet it is, he notes, highly contagious, and it is quite possible for whites to become infected. He reports that "a white woman in North Carolina not only acquired a dark color, but several of the features of a Negro, by marrying and living with a black husband."[24] (There is no mention, curiously enough, of whether this physical change was observed in white men who cohabitated with black women.) The contagious nature of the disease of blackness required that black people be quarantined. Dr. Rush argued that it was necessary to separate the races for reasons of public health. The creation of huge racial leper colonies was only a temporary measure. The final remedy, according to Rush, was to cure black people of their blackness. Only by turning their skin white could people of African descent be healed of their infirmity. Dr. Rush recommended the ancient practice of bleeding, or purging, to accomplish this task.

The rhetoric of disease was not always associated with the physical color of the African's skin. Black people were also thought to suffer from a variety of mental diseases.

> One of the interesting sidelights of [this issue] was triggered by the sixth national census of 1840. When the results were published in 1841, it was for the first time possible to obtain data concerning mental illness in the United States. The total number of those reported to be insane and feeble-minded in the United States was over 17,000, of which nearly 3,000 were black. If these staggering census statistics were to be believed, free blacks had an incidence of mental illness eleven times higher than slaves and six times higher than the white population. The antiabolitionist forces were thus provided with major scientific evidence that blacks were congenitally unfit for freedom.[25]

In 1851, as scientific theories of racial inferiority emerged, Samuel Cartwright published a paper in the *New Orleans Surgical Journal*, in which he identified certain psychopathologies to which black people, alone, were prey. Chief among these was "Drapetomania," a disease which caused black slaves to run away.[26] The desire to be free and resistance to the institution of slavery was thus diagnosed as a mental illness. The function of slavery were to cure black people of this condition. Many people in the medical profession saw black people as a disease in the body politic. Only when that disease had been eradicated could the nation reach its full destiny.

One of the lesser observed sources of the rhetoric of disease as blackness is found in the theological discourse of early and medieval Christianity. The propensity of early Christian writers to employ the racially charged symbols of blackness and whiteness to denote evil and good, disease and health, is well documented. Much of this discourse was set by the commentaries of St. Ambrose of Milan and St. Bernard of Clairvaux on the Song of Songs. In reading that particular book of the Bible both assume that the color of the Shulamite maiden is a sign of her fall from grace. Blackness is associated with sin, and sin is associated with disease. It is also permissible, however, in this line of thought, to sacrifice the body of black people to enhance the health of white people. One of the most revered legends within the medieval church involved the twin physicians, Cosmas and Damian:

> Born in Cilicia in the third century, they were physicians who in the hope of gaining converts to Christianity provided their services without fee. They suffered a grotesque martyrdom in the year 278 during the reign of Diocletian but soon gained a following, at first in the East and later in the West, for numerous miraculous cures both in life and after death. . . . Their most famous miracle occurred at a church named after them in a formerly pagan temple at the edge of the Forum in Rome, where they appeared posthumously to replace the gangrenous leg of the church's sacristan with the leg of a Negro who had died of old age.[27]

Not only does this legend buttress the unspoken assumption that the bodies of black persons can be sacrificed for the health of white persons, there is an interesting twist given to this story in a sixteenth-century painting attributed to Fernando del Rincon, depicting this famous miracle. In this painting not only does the sacristan have the healthy leg of the black person grafted onto his body, but lying on the floor we see the black man with the diseased white leg grafted onto his body. It is this unspoken and almost unconscious assumption that the black body can serve as a kind of ritual victim who bears the sin of disease that lends complexity to the rhetoric of disease as blackness. Theophus H. Smith argues convincingly that black people have functioned in American religious discourse as a *"pharmakon."*[28] A pharmakon can be both a poison and a cure, a sign of disease and an avenue to health as purity.

Such categories of health and disease furnished a powerful set of metaphors and binary oppositions for a culture radically divided by race. The idea of disease is deeply rooted in the history of human attempts to make sense of the unknown. The Tuskegee Experiment simply confirmed the historical assumption that black bodies could be sacrificed for the health of others. The debate on providing health care to every American citizen resurrected the submerged language of health and disease. It was a debate that could not be solved at the policy level, because it raised much deeper questions. Who shall be saved from this disease called sin? How shall we be saved? Who shall heal our sin-sick souls?

Health and Disease in the Bible

Within the history of medical thought in the West a rhetoric of disease emerged. This rhetoric persisted through the rationalistic development of medical thought and practice because it provided a way to account for the strange and unknown in human experience. In the course of time, that rhetoric became associated with people of African descent. The association was buttressed by Western philosophical and cultural discourse and by certain aspects of Western Christian narratives. The system of chattel slavery in the United States also found support in this rhetoric of disease, because black skin was deemed pathological. The question which confronts us at this juncture is: What are the resources which the Bible offers to counter this rhetoric of disease, especially in its association with blackness?

The contribution of the Hebrew Scriptures to this topic is found in its purity codes and its hygenic restrictions, and also in its focus on the relationship between health and wholeness. The dietary and sanitary restrictions found in the Pentateuch and described in the older commentaries stress that these mandates had their source and ultimate purpose in obedience to God. Later scholars, however, have argued that the Israelite dietary restrictions against eating certain animals had a basis in the maintenance of human health and prevention of disease. In addition, the practice of circumcision is, at least in this view, not only an act of obedience to God but also recognized by the medical profession as good preventive medicine. One could point to the biblical injunctions requiring those who are diseased to remain separate from the community as a form of quarantine, or to the command for the ritual washing of the hands as a good antiseptic practice. Such emphasis on showing that the mandates of the Hebrew Bible are consistent with good secular medical practice is more meaningful to those for whom good medical care is readily available, but it says little to those whose lives are circumscribed by the rhetoric of disease.

A more critical perspective on the origin and derivation of these biblical mandates would recognize that, in all likelihood, the Israelites inherited a number of their beliefs about disease from ancient Mesopotamian cultures.[29] Putting the biblical mandates regarding dietary restrictions in a broader social context might yield a different perspective on their origin and function.

The ideas of health and disease in the Hebrew Bible must be understood in the individual contexts in which they are raised. This means that health, as defined in the Mosaic Law, is similar to the description adopted by the World Health Association in 1946. Health is "a state of complete well-being and not merely the absence of disease or infirmity."[30] In the Hebrew Bible, health involves the unity of the mind, body, and spirit. "The healthy person is the person who exhibits physical, mental, and spiritual wholeness. This sense of wholeness, of *shalom*, of well-being, is not confined merely to the individual person, but extends beyond the individual to the community as well. The healthy person is an integral part of the community."[31] Health and disease are complex notions in the Hebrew Bible. Health is not merely the absence of affliction; it involves a unique quality of life. Disease cannot be explained simply as divine punishment for sin—a common belief among ancient Mesopotamian cultures—as the story of Job reveals. It is an indeterminate aspect of human experience that derives its meaning, in large part, from its context.

The principal biblical resources that have traditionally been used to address questions of health and disease have been found in the New Testament. Here the presence of disease is often associated with questions of theodicy. Within the New Testament is evidence for at least six different explanations for infirmity.[32] The first is possession by demons or evil spirits (Luke 13:10-17). The second explanation is that God has inflicted disease to punish the sufferer for his or her sins (John 5:1-15). The third is that it may be punishment for the sins of one's parents (John 9:3). The fourth is that it may be punishment for sins in a past life (John 9:3). The fifth is that disease may be permitted to show God's power to heal (John 9:3). And the sixth is that disease may be permitted to show God's power to sustain the sufferer even if the disease is not healed. Beneath the textual evidence supporting these explanations of illness in the New Testament lie deeper issues that are important to understanding the revolutionary significance of Jesus' healing ministry.

In the field of medical anthropology crucial distinctions are made between disease, illness, and sickness. One of the most influential writers in the field describes them in the following manner. "*Disease* refers to abnormalities in the structure and/or function of organs and organ systems; pathological states whether or not they are culturally recognized. . . . *Illness* refers to a person's perceptions and experiences of certain socially disvalued states including, but not limited to, disease. *Sickness* is a blanket term to label events involving disease and/or illness."[33] The key to these definitions is that disease refers to some inherent abnormality in the person. Both illness and sickness include a focus on the subjectivity of the sufferer. Most definitions of disease, illness, and sickness in the field of medical anthropology share this emphasis on disease as a thing that overshadows or renders meaningless the subjectivity of the sufferer. Illness and sickness are determined by asking the patient how he or she feels in anticipation of treatment. Disease is associated with some external and observable feature of the person. Here the subjectivity of the sufferer is obscured and quarantine is prescribed. This explains the tendency of some New Testament scholars to discount the significance of the category of disease and to emphasize illness as the most appropriate concept related to healing and health.[34] It is my contention, however, that it is *disease,* with all of its connotations and effects, that Jesus addresses in his ministry of healing. The character of disease is that it removes the person from the community. It prevents wholeness and solidarity among people. It overshadows the personhood of the sufferer. It consigns the sufferer to an existence within the company of the afflicted. This is why Jesus never looked down on or shunned the sufferers of disease. In many of his healing miracles he brought the sufferer of disease into community. Those who are ill or sick elicit compassion because they are recognized as human beings by others in the community. Thus one way to understand the healing ministry of Jesus is that he takes disease and removes the stigma associated with it, so that the person is seen as simply ill or sick and therefore deserving of compassion and treatment. The oppressive nature of the physical condition of the sufferer is alleviated, and true healing can begin to take place.

The disease most often explicitly named in the New Testament is leprosy. Jesus' willingness to approach those suffering from this dreaded disease is even more significant in light of the stigma involved. Most biblical scholars agree that what is called "leprosy" was not one thing but a name for a variety of symptomatic conditions all of which were associated with the skin. This points to the function of disease in any culture. It does not invite close investigation. It is a marker for that of which we are afraid. (While AIDS is caused by a single HIV virus, some scholars have observed that AIDS is the name for a variety of observable symptoms.) This is the reason that black people have been associated with dreaded diseases since at least the sixth century. What African Americans find in the miraculous healing ministry of Jesus is a way out of the company of the afflicted and into the community of the redeemed.

The Bible provides resources for the deconstruction of the rhetoric of disease that has often attended the experience of people of African descent. The Bible does not give a definitive answer to the question of why disease afflicts some and not others. Even Jesus does not attempt to explain the presence of disease. He simply affirms that as creations of God the sufferers of disease are promised wholeness and salvation. Jesus brought hope, dignity, and liberation to the sick and afflicted. His ministry of healing is central to a revision of our understanding of the meaning of salvation. This brings us to the final task of this chapter, that is, articulating a proposal for revising our theological understanding of salvation.

Is There a Balm in Gilead?

African American Christians have creatively used the resources at hand to articulate an understanding of salvation suited to their own circumstances. Those resources include traditional Western notions of salvation, and notions of healing in African traditional religions and African Christianity. The blend of these elements in the unique context of the experience of black people in the New World has yielded new insights into the nature of health and salvation.

One of the more perplexing questions in the history of Western Christian thought concerns the rationale for the salvation of humanity. Since at least the time of Athanasius, soteriology has been intimately connected with Christology in Christian thought. That is, questions of the salvation of humanity are wound up in questions of the identity of Jesus Christ. Within the variety of older theories of salvation, there is involved a commerce between Jesus Christ and God. It is the mystery of this interaction which gives rise to, and ultimately, supersedes each theory. The *ransom theory*, associated with Origen and Gregory of

Nyssa, held that humanity had wandered away from God and had fallen into the hands of the devil, who demanded a price for the release of humankind. The price demanded was the blood of Christ. The *satisfaction theory*, associated primarily with Anselm, proposed that by sinning humanity had dishonored God. Only the life of Jesus Christ could restore that honor. The *moral or exemplarist theory*, generally associated with Peter Abelard, held that the purpose of the life and death of Christ was to model the righteousness and love that is inherent in humanity. The *penal or judicial theory*, which emerged in the Reformation period and is associated with John Calvin and Hugo Grotius, proposed that human sin was a crime for which the justice of God demanded punishment. In this theory Christ accepted the guilty verdict for us. The *sacrificial theory*, which is consistently present in Western Christian thought from the time of Augustine through the Middle Ages to the Enlightenment, asserted that the forgiveness of human sin required a blood sacrifice. Jesus Christ, the lamb without spot, was therefore slain for our transgressions. The goal of the salvific act has been described in numerous ways. It is the deification of humanity, the imputation of righteousness before God, union with Christ, moral perfection, authentic humanity, and political liberation, among others. They all point to the removal of the barriers between God and humanity as requisite for human wholeness and well-being. Most modern notions of salvation also point in this direction. Karl Barth's *reconciliation,* Rudolf Bultmann's *authentic existence,* Reinhold Niebuhr's *restoration of original justice,* Paul Tillich's *participation in New Being,* Karl Rahner's *self-offering of God to the world,* Gustavo Gutiérrez' *liberation from class oppression,* and Rosemary Radford Ruether's *original wholeness of humanity as found in Mary,* all imply the reconnection of humanity with God. All of these theories of salvation, however, both ancient and modern, focus on the effects of sin upon the sinners. This is an element of the doctrine of salvation that has found a home in African American Christian thought. But African American Christians have asked more of soteriology. They have asked not only what salvation means to the sinner, but also, What does salvation mean to the victims of sin?

Salvation in African American Experience

In African traditional and African Christian thought, health is understood as harmony and disease as disharmony. One African writer notes that in African traditional thought, "Any sickness [is] viewed not only as a threat to one's existence but also as a distabilisation of cosmic harmony, as there was no real distinction made between the natural and the supernatural."[35] In African traditional as well as African Christian thought, health and disease are intimately associated with matters of the spirit. There is an overriding belief in the spiritual causation of illness, even while acknowledging the efficacy of Western medical innovations and practices. The spirit is not only involved in the causation of disease but, in African Christian thought, also in healing. The role of the Holy Spirit has been central to the self-understanding of many indigenous African churches. Among African Pentecostal churches the power of the Holy Spirit effects healing by defeating the spiritual causes of illness. This healing includes "not just bodily recuperation, but finding remedies for unemployment, family disputes, racism, marital discord, and controversies between factions in a tribe or village."[36] In African traditional thought the sick person is not simply a subdued recipient of medical treatment. In this view "the sick person is seen not as a passive 'patient,' the suffering object of the active therapist or as the determined occupant of a 'sick role,' but as an agent, a subject seeking health, engaged . . . in a 'quest for therapy,' in problem solving, and manipulating the resources available in the environment—and, if need be, changing that environment."[37] On this quest for therapy, the patient might seek a number of treatments, including the use of herbs, ritual cleansing, and incantations or prayers. In African traditional thought, the concept of salvation as healing focuses on the plight of the victim of disease and with the alleviation of the suffering which accompanies it. This is often done by attempting to placate the offended spirits. But African American Christians have asked more of the notion of healing: In what way does human healing reflect God's providential care, through the power of the Holy Spirit, of the entire created order?

James Lapsley, Donald Bloesch, among others have argued, convincingly, that health and salvation, or health and forgiveness, are not synonymous.[38] Not everyone who enjoys health will be saved. Not everyone who is saved will enjoy physical health. Health and salvation are, however, related terms. Within the context of a rhetoric of disease as blackness, both ideas need to be revised.

Health, as symbolized by access to quality health care, has become in our time a privatized commodity. It has lost its social, communal, and covenantal character. "This loss of shared public understandings of health contributes to an unhealthy national and international situation in which consumer expectations converge and contend over costly resources."[39] The pursuit of perfect health has raised the volume of discussions of health care but has also skewed its role and importance in human existence. The fact that health is not synonymous with salvation or forgiveness suggests that health, like salvation, is a gift. Health is a relative term; it is not to be thought of as some ideal human condition. Health, while important, is only one aspect of a life worth living. A spiritually balanced life seeks harmony. A measure of good health is valuable to the degree that it allows one to give glory to God. This is why traditional prayers in African American Christian worship will often begin by thanking God "for a reasonable portion of health and strength. Thank you for letting me awake this morning clothed in my right mind, with the blood running warm in my veins." Health is a penultimate good. Life in the presence of God is the ultimate good.

Salvation, like health, is a gift from God. Yet salvation has become a private affair, referring to the redemption of the individual from guilt, despair, fear, and death. But salvation is social because sin is social. The social character of sin is not simply its manifestation in institutions. Theologians like Walter Rauschenbusch highlighted this aspect of sin through the Social Gospel. Sin is social because the sin of an individual is not just an offense to God; it injures other people. The social character of salvation is not merely its focus on groups. The notion of salvation in the Hebrew Bible emphasized this aspect of redemption. Salvation is social because the redemption of the victims of sin can be the avenue through which those whose sinfulness wreaks havoc in the world are also saved. This means that the description of salvation must include those who are wounded by sin. In African American experience salvation is not escape from the challenges of creaturely existence. Redemption is not exemption. In African American experience, racism is recognized as a cultural pathology. In spite of an environment created by the rhetoric of disease as blackness, people of African descent have always known that they are the victims of the pathology of racism, and not the carriers of social disease. This knowledge is encoded in the cultural form of the blues. (There is a striking similarity between the blues in African American experience, and *han* in the experience of Korean Christians. This similarity has led to a view on the nature of salvation that is quite compatible with that described here. Andrew Sung Park observes that "in the efforts to heal the victims of their sins or the sins of others, sinners can experience salvation. . . . The idea that sinners can achieve salvation by confessing their own sin regardless of the welfare of their victims is a narcissistic illusion.")[40] In the blues, awareness of one's status as a victim of racism is the first step toward transcending that status. Diagnosis of the association of blackness and disease is the first step toward the therapeutic affirmation that blackness is healthy.

Salvation as healing is a central concern in African American Christianity. In at least three ways this salvation is experienced and draws upon traditions of African healing and Western soteriology. First, *salvation occurs through the prayers of the faithful.* It recalls the incantations used in African healing and combines it with the salvific power of the Word in Reformation theology. Prayer is essential to salvation as health, because it overcomes the alienating affects of disease by bringing the victims into union with God. Second, *salvation occurs through the gathered community of faith.* It recalls the ecstatic presence of the spirit experienced by the collective group in African traditional healing rituals and combines it with the patristic emphasis on the church as the means of salvation. The worshiping community enables, sustains, confirms, and shares in the healing of its members and thereby becomes the means of salvation. Third, *salvation occurs through the sacraments or ordinances of the Lord's Supper and Baptism.* It recalls the use of herbal medicines and ritual bathing as healing practices in African traditional religions and combines them with ancient Christian views on the efficacy of bread, wine, and water. These ritual practices emphasize the participation of each member of the community in the salvific presence of Christ.

Salvation and health are interrelated in human experience. This is because the notion of disease continues to function as a symbol for what we do not understand. The limits of Western medicine are evident in "the appearance of new strains of disease and of disease carriers . . . of diseases generated by alterations in the environment . . . and the inability of doctors to deal with the social sources of illness . . . [and] the appearance even of new 'diseases of affluence.'"[41] Healing will continue to occupy the imagination of the Christian community for reasons other than the failures of modern medicine, however. Healing brings to the fore the power of the salvation of God and serves evangelistic purposes. F. D. Bruner states that "nothing attracts men and attests the Gospel . . . quite like the healing of infirmities. Indeed healing fills out the full gospel of a full salvation. . . ."[42]

In African American worship the references to Jesus as the restorer of health and wholeness are numerous. "Jesus is a doctor who has never lost a patient." "Jesus is the one who gives me all my medicine." "Jesus is the balm in Gilead to heal the sin-sick soul." In a society where the means to health have become a commodity ruled by the marketplace, and where people of African descent have too often found themselves circumscribed by the rhetoric of disease, salvation must mean more than escape from the natural processes of living and dying. Salvation must give ultimate meaning to life itself. The work of theology and ministry must proclaim the availability and power of salvation as health and wholeness for our times.

Hope, Racism, and Community

*But hope that is seen is no hope at all. Who hopes
for what they already have? But if we hope for
what we do not yet have, we wait for it patiently.*
—Romans 8:24-25

During the nineteenth century the industrial juggernaut of the Western world roared to life and with it the promise of common prosperity. What was utopia to some, however, was Armageddon to others. People living in the United States then were beset by a host of secular eschatologies, that is, religiously charged visions of the future. Some of these secular eschatologies gave hope to the underclasses. (In Christian theological discourse, eschatology refers to the "doctrine of last things." The term has come to be associated, however, with the general notion of human destiny, the future of the crested order, and the world to come.) Marxism had its appeal to the working classes. Various agrarian reform movements spoke to those being systematically removed from the land. Socialist and communitarian groups searched for the restoration of pre-capitalist social values. Many of these movements were and remain legitimate expressions of human longing for freedom and wholeness, while others function as cultural spin-offs of the idea of Christian hope. These secular eschatologies normally appeal to the universal hope for a brighter future (lotteries and gambling are two of the modalities through which this hope is commonly pursued today) or a deep-seated desire to return to "the good old days" (an impulse aptly captured in the phrase "back to the future"). In this way secular eschatologies address the alienation and disorientation that seemed to accompany the rise of the modern industrial state.

While there has scarcely been an industrialized nation that has not been funded by some pseudo-eschatological vision, the United States has been profoundly shaped by notions of the future. H. Richard Niebuhr's *The Kingdom of God in America* and Max Weber's *The Protestant Ethic and the Spirit of Capitalism* examine this aspect of the national consciousness. Eschatological thinking has been influenced by the modern notion of progress. At the same time there also lingers the persistent suspicion that history is dynamic but not necessarily progressive. Part of the complexity of American life is the variety of visions of the future expressed in public, political, religious, and cultural institutions. One such eschatological vision is that found in the cultural practices and institutions of those groups which are labeled as "white supremacists." White supremacy is a virulent and persistent strain in American social life. Its root system runs deep into the soil of Western culture. In the United States it has been sustained by a dubious relation to Christian doctrine and practice. The major concern in the following discussion is the relationship between Christian eschatology and the fundamental vision of white supremacy. We will examine the convergence and conflict between the ideological basis of Christianity and those groups for whom the white race is the ultimate measure of humanity. Most North American Christians would not be very comfortable the association of the vision of the future found in white supremacy and Christian eschatology. Yet in its light we are presented with the opportunity to examine the fundamental concepts, ideas, tropes, and metaphors in traditional Christian eschatology, and to assess their appropriateness for theological discourse today.

Eschatology in Modern Theology

Eschatology means literally "discourse about last things." It refers to that branch of systematic theology which has normally encompassed reflections on the immortality of the soul, the resurrection of the body, eternal judgment, and heaven and hell. It also includes discussions of purgatory, limbo, and the beatific vision. In early Israel, eschatological discourse concerned the establishment of the reign of God on earth. Justice, peace, prosperity, and orderly government were viewed as possibilities within history. In later Judaism the disappointments that followed the failure of the promise of national tranquility found expression in the apocalyptic images of the prophetic writings of the Bible. In the New Testament the explicit apocalyptic of the prophetic writings served as a backdrop for the proclamation of the coming reign of God, the resurrection of the body, eternal judgment, and salvation. In fact, without the gloss put on the texts by subsequent interpreters, one might say that the ministry and mission of Jesus was driven by his eschatological consciousness. This consciousness was concretized in Jesus' proclamation of God's "reign" or *basileia*. A central metaphor for this reality is that of the *beloved community*. This notion has become deeply rooted both in the memory of the early church through the writings of Irenaeus, and in the cultural consciousness of the United States through the writings of Jonathan Edwards.[1]

Eschatology became a central concern for the Christian community early in its existence. The delayed *parousia* or return of Jesus and its implications for the faith had to be dealt with while preserving the promissory foundation of the gospel. Yet the early church managed to maintain its self-understanding as a beloved community in Christ. Two major events in the subsequent history of the church profoundly affected the church's self-concept. The first was the legitimation of the church by the Emperor Constantine, followed by Augustine's redefinition of the church from "beloved community" to "the City of God." This move from *communitas* to *polis* introduced radically different notions of social organization within the church. The second event was the emergence of feudal society and Thomas Aquinas' intellectual reconstruction of the medieval church along those lines. Within the emergent hierarchical structure of the church certain class distinctions became codified and identified with normative church order. As a result of both of these events, the communal eschatological consciousness so evident in the early church went underground.

In the modern era a variety of theological positions on the meaning of eschatology emerged. The classical liberal theologies which dominated theological reflection from the beginning of the eighteenth century until the outbreak of World War I translated the eschatological thrust of the Bible into various notions of progress. Jesus' sayings regarding the coming reign of God were taken to mean that human and social perfection were not only possible in history but quite inevitable. Human beings as well as their social and cultural institutions were ordained for fulfillment rather than destruction. The seeds of that perfection were planted in the act of creation, and only ignorance could alter their course toward their destiny. The basic assumption was that God was at work in the world employing human talents and genius to complete God's design for the world. Behind this translation was the conviction that the eschatology of the Bible, and especially the expressive vehicle of apocalyptic imagery, were part of an outmoded cosmology foreign to the modern world. The neo-orthodox theologians, who gained prominence after the outbreak of World War I, sought to reclaim part of the gospel content that had been jettisoned by their liberal forebears, especially the doctrine of sin. The human slaughter that characterized modern warfare and the appearance of social phenomena that had no explanation outside of the notion of radical evil, convinced these theologians that human beings and their institutions were not on a collision course with perfection. Rather, human beings were infinitely capable of deceiving themselves, of hiding their true motives behind ingenious veneers, in other words, of sin. Human institutions were easily corrupted by the pursuit of power, and human history was shot through with tragedy and irony. In light of these factors neo-orthodox theologians attempted to reclaim the elements of judgment and redemption in Christian eschatology. But neo-orthodox theologians were also part of the modern world inhabited by their liberal counterparts. Therefore it was impossible simply to present the first-century eschatology of the Bible to a world struggling with modern methods of madness and mayhem. They could not, in good conscience, claim that the course of history would be miraculously interrupted and a new reality inaugurated. Thus, they posited a theory of two historical realities, sacred history (*heilgeschichte*), and human history (*weltgeschichte*). The eschatological moment, then, occurred whenever one became aware of the judgment, condemnation, and affirmation which the history of salvation rendered upon human history. Thus apocalyptic language became symbolic of the distance between human work in history and God's work in history.

In addition to liberal and neo-orthodox strands in Christian theology, several others have contributed to eschatological thinking. In process theology, the central problematic is the conflict between the claim that God is benevolent and omnipotent, and the presence of radical evil. This issue is the guide to the development of the major emphases in process thought. The notion of eschatology in process theology points to the resolution of its initial problematic, that is, the end of evil, harmony within the Godhead, and in the human community.[2] In various forms of political theology, eschatology has had an important place, but none more central than in the theology of hope.[3] These theologians argue that eschatology, rather than serving as an addendum to systematic theology, should be its axiomatic principle. The Christian community, humanity as a whole, and the church's affirmation of Jesus Christ as the Son of God, can only be adequately understood in light of the future from which God calls. In this theology, the reversals and disappointments that are part of historical reality must be set in the context of a future over which God exercises complete sovereignty. In the development of liberation theology, especially in Latin America, eschatology played an important, though undervalued, role.[4] Although most observers focused on the use of Marxist social analysis by many Latin American theologians, at the heart of much of this theology was a utopian vision of the future. This vision was often couched in social language referring to "a classless society" or "a liberated existence for the poor." Yet this eschatological vision was as much spiritual as it was political. Contemporary feminist theologians have identified the ways that gender has influenced the development of Christian eschatology. Rosemary Radford Ruether argues that the traditional trajectory of eschatology as "an endless flight into an unrealized future" needs to be replaced by a model of *conversion*.[5] In this instance, the end of human existence is wholeness and balanced relationships between persons, and between people and the nonhuman environment. In black theology in the United States the role of eschatology has been controversial, ambivalent, and contested. The highly ornate descriptions of heaven and the future in the afterlife in African American folklore have raised questions as to whether this vision was helpful or harmful to a people struggling for health, liberation, and wholeness in *this* world.[6] The consensus among African American male theologians and womanist theologians is that although the eschatological consciousness of black people has been abused in the past, it has more often given sustenance to a people struggling for freedom.

The development of eschatology in Christian theology since the beginning of the eighteenth century has been defined by the requirement to reconcile the claims of biblical religion to the demands of the modern ethos. Theological positions emerging during this period have responded to this mandate in somewhat different ways. Some have adjusted their understanding of the Christian faith to the demands of modernity, while others have employed biblical faith to critique the modernist spirit. A common feature in all of these positions, however, is the diminution of the prominence of apocalyptic imagery in eschato-logical discourse.

As a result, apocalyptic imagery has been employed primarily in mil-lennialist forms of eschatological discourse. The political origins of apocalyptic imagery are found in the biblical accounts of Jewish histo-ry. In those periods when the Jewish people felt threatened by a loss of national security, expectations that God would dramatically intervene in history on their behalf abounded. This intervention would inaugu-rate the reign of God. During these times apocalyptic ideas and litera-ture emerged. These images of the cataclysmic confrontation between the powers of good and evil depicted more than the Jewish quest for righteousness. They also referred to the political and military hopes of an oppressed people. They lived in a world thought to be dominated by evil forces, and it would take more than human effort alone to ban-ish them. The overthrow of the reign of evil would then issue forth an age of bliss and tranquility. Since the conditions that originally gave rise to apocalyptic literature were still prevalent during the time of Jesus it is reasonable to assume that these ideas formed the backdrop of Jesus' preaching and ministry. The texts of the New Testament reflect this fact in that these ideas and images are found in the three Synoptic Gospels and in the Book of Revelation.

A key element in apocalyptic discourse is millennialism. Millennial-ism refers to the belief in a thousand-year reign of Christ in which the reign of God is brought to fruition. There are two major varieties of millennialist thinking. Premillennialism is the conviction that the Sec-ond Coming of Christ will precede the thousand-year reign of Christ. Postmillennialism is the conviction that the coming of Christ will fol-low the millennium. The former belief includes a chronology in which tribulation and strife will mark the coming of the Anti-Christ. This is followed by the thousand-year reign of peace and order, which is then followed by the catastrophic battle between good and evil and the final victory of Christ. Postmillennialists, on the other hand, have generally identified the reign of Christ with the age of the church, which will be followed by the conflict between good and evil, and the Second Com-ing of Christ.

Milliennialist thought took root in the United States during the period of the American Revolution and the Second Great Awakening. The establishment of a new political state and the quest for moral per-fection were initially collapsed in an attempt to proclaim the dawning of a new age. The political pragmatism required to preserve and advance the emerging nation stood in stark contrast, however, with the religious idealism at the heart of the quest for personal perfection. Moreover, those groups which held most securely millennialist views— Shakers, Oneida Perfectionists, Seventh-Day Adventists, and Mormons—soon found themselves marginal participants in the discourse which shaped the identity of the nation. The last major thrust of millennialist activity in the social life of the United States occurred in 1844. William Miller, a Baptist and the author of *Evidence from Scripture and History of the Second Coming of Christ, about the Year 1843*, published in 1836, calculated that Christ would return to earth between March 21, 1843, and March 21, 1844. When Christ did not appear by the appointed date, a new date of October 22, 1844, was set. When this date also came and went, Miller's disillusioned followers dispersed, and millennialist thought went underground.

The Rise of White Supremacy in the United States

It is unclear whether slavery in the United States was the cause or result of the rise of white supremacy. Evidence seems to suggest, however, that the systemic forces that sustained the enslavement of Africans derived their impetus from the vortex of classism and racism. George M. Frederickson, in his study *White Supremacy: A Comparative Study in American and South African History*, observes that "the participation of lower-class whites in these disorders was induced to a great extent by the status anxieties generated by a competitive society. For those who had little chance to realize the American dream of upward mobility, it was comforting to think there was a clearly defined out-group that was even lower in the social hierarchy."[7] Within the sectional conflict that erupted into civil war were competing views of the optimum social order. In the North, the argument was that the social order should be based on achievement rather than "ascription." Therefore, the principle which stated that Africans were naturally destined to be slaves was opposed. This did not mean that the natural equality of Africans was affirmed but rather that the basis for asserting their inequality was their supposed inferior levels of intellectual, moral, and cultural achievement. In the South, the argument was that the social order should be based on a kind of natural law that placed the master class in positions of power and responsibility. It was therefore possible that individual instances of genius and creativity among African slaves could be recognized and even applauded without rendering a challenge to the cosmic laws that relegated them to a "mudsill" class.

As the still-fledgling nation struggled to forge an identity, both the North and the South faced the specter of an overthrow of the basis of their social order. In the South, resistance to the abolition of slavery rested on the conviction that an inevitable race struggle would result. In the North, resistance to the full participation of Africans in the economic development of the region rested on the conviction that something akin to a class struggle would be inevitable. In both instances, ample cause for white supremacist attitudes could be found. Yet it was in the South that the economic factors during and after the Civil War made white supremacy the centerpiece of the social order. The political structure of Southern society—including the disempowerment and disenfranchisement of African Americans—after the Civil War suggests that the economic development of the South created a complex ideological system of race and class relations which left black people at the bottom of the heap.[8]

The final three decades of the twentieth century have witnessed the reemergence of various white supremacist groups. Although the ideas and sentiments that sustain these racist attitudes have never been far from the surface of American social and political life, at clearly identifiable moments in history they have coalesced, challenging the stated philosophical foundations of U.S. society. In recent years several groups with otherwise different agendas have found common cause in the idea of white supremacy. Among them are survivalists, tax resisters, white nationalists, counterfeiters, Christian home educators, anti-abortionists, gun enthusiasts, mercenary afficionados, and neoconservatives.[9] This broad, loosely related consortium of racists includes the more familiar coalition of groups in the Ku Klux Klan, the American Nazi Party, and the John Birch Society, as well as such lesser-known groups as the Liberty Lobby, the American Front, the Covenant, the Sword, and the Arm of the Lord (CSA), and the Populist Party. The sobering economic, global, and political realities of the latter part of the century were the catalyst for the formation of "a new phase in the far-right movement, which would come to be known as the Fifth Era."[10] This new age would see the creation or, more accurately, the re-creation of the nation. It would be "an America Christian and masculine in its culture, racially white, English-speaking, and overseen by its sacred compact, the United States Constitution."[11] For our purposes several of the groups in this "silent brotherhood"[12] warrant further description.

The Ku Klux Klan had its origins in the aftermath of the Civil War:

In Pulaski, Tennessee in 1866, half a dozen recently returned—and bored—Confederate soldiers who were looking around for a source of amusement formed an organization they called the Ku Klux Klan. Members would turn up at town gatherings dressed in outlandish outfits and publicly hazed their newest recruits. They put together a group for playing practical jokes, like draping themselves in sheets and wandering about town, spooking the public. These early Kluxers had no political consciousness at all; their only stated purpose was "to have fun, make mischief, and play pranks on the public." But soon they turned to newly freed blacks as a source of humor, recounting stories of how their nighttime hijinks frightened the freedmen. As its reputation for merry pranks grew, the Klan took on the trappings of a full-fledged civic organization.[13]

As the Klan developed, many of its internal ceremonies were modeled on church ritual. A particular target group for Klan recruiters were ministers. Later, the Klan sought to position itself as a defender of common piety, "appealing to nativist intolerance, fundamentalist frustration with the libertinism of the Roaring Twenties, and the general antimodernist urge of the heartland."[14] Since its beginning, the Klan has waxed and waned as an influence in American life during the five discernible periods in the evolution of its organization.

Its First Era, during post-Civil War radical reconstruction, saw an insurgent outlaw army. It soon withered, then rose again in a Second Era in the 1920s, an above-ground political phase that attracted millions of members. The Third Era was a violent, rear-guard battle against the civil rights movement of the 1960s. The Fourth Era in the 1970s, was a public relations campaign, led most importantly by the young David Duke, who would go on to become a member of the Louisiana state legislature and, in 1990, make a run for the U.S. Senate. The Fifth Era, in the 1980s and beyond, involves both an armed underground and an aggressive above-board political movement.[15]

The Aryan Nations, the Order, and the White Aryan Resistance are interlocking groups which share a common theme of racial purity and armed resistance to the federal government. The Aryan Nations, also known as the Church of Jesus Christ Christian, was the vehicle through which several white supremacist groups forged their vision of the future of America. By drawing on the religious fervor, political frustration, and xenophobia of much of the European-American populace, the leaders of this organization formulated a three-pronged plan "to make National Socialism the next high Christian culture in America."[16] An international Aryan Congress would be held every year, at which major white supremacists would be invited to speak. Second, a direct solicitation campaign would be initiated to enlist others who might share a general opposition to current liberal social and governmental trends. Third, special attention would be paid to the recruitment of whites among the prison population, where the forces of separatism among racial groups was already strong.

The Order was a splinter group of the Aryan Nations. The first meeting of the Order was held in the summer of 1983 and included members of the Aryan Nations church who were not content with wearing swastikas and uttering the name of Adolf Hitler. Also present were members of the Ku Klux Klan who wanted action and not rhetoric. In essence, the Order was an underground terrorist group of the far right. Its members were implicated in the murder of a Jewish radio talk show host in Denver, Colorado, who regularly criticized white supremacist groups, as well as in several robberies of banks and armored cars. They passed counterfeit currency and engaged in a host of other illegal activities to finance their racial revolution.

The White Aryan Resistance (WAR) represents the maturation of the Aryan supremacist movement. Its leader, rather than employing inflammatory rhetoric, states the racist premises of the movement with a kind of matter-of-factness. The focus is on discipline rather than anarchy, and its major target is young people. This does not mean that WAR is any less firm in its racist intentions than other groups. It simply means that this group has adopted modern methods of appeal and recruitment.[17]

While many white supremacist groups demonstrated a contempt for the law, one major group was founded on the principle of the conservation of law and order, the Posse Comitatus:

> The Posse Comitatus was first organized in Portland, Oregon in 1969 by Henry L. Beach, who had just retired from the dry cleaning business. During the 1930s Beach was the state liaison officer for William Dudley Pelley's Silver Shirts, the storm trooper group formed immediately after Hitler took power in Germany. The Posse believes all politics are local. Beach argued that the county sheriff is the highest legitimately elected official in the land, and that the sheriff has the right to form a posse including any able-bodied man over the age of eighteen. To the Posse the sheriff is, in reality, the executive branch of government. He directs law enforcement, including the enpanelling of juries.[18]

As a constitutional fundamentalist group the Posse Comitatus believes that the federal government has exceeded the limits of the Constitution and therefore has violated the inalienable rights of its citizens. Government intervention into education, the coining of money not based on the gold or silver standard, the establishment of the Federal Reserve, the federal attempt to regulate the sale and possession of handguns, and the U.S. role in the affairs of other nations, are examples of this violation. Many Posse members believe that the nation has gone too far toward socialism and world government. Posse members claim that the Constitution establishes individual states as "separate sovereign Republics within the United States."[19] Therefore federal income taxation is a violation of the right to local government. Belief in the power of each locality to establish its own law has been one of the mainstays of white supremacy. Unwarranted incarceration, harassment, and even lynchings of black people have been justified by appeal to it. Here the xenophobia which many white supremacist groups share has found expression in the alleged constitutional right to self-rule.[20] These groups, along with the White Patriot Party, the American Nazi Party, and the John Birch Society, among others, have carried the banner of white supremacism in the United States and abroad.

As George Kelsey pointed out, these groups are determined to provide a basis for solidarity among a race which has sensed a loss of community. This is most expeditiously accomplished by targeting certain other racial groups as threats to order and civility. "By positing an enemy race, the racist ideology produces cohesion within white society. At this point, the ideology is a call to vigilance, and if need be, to attack."[21]

Although Roman Catholics and various immigrant groups have been among the targets of white supremacist groups in the United States, African Americans and Jewish people have been singled out as primary recipients of racist venom. Attacks on Jewish people are based on a complex myth in which Jewish people are accused of carrying out a massive conspiracy to control the world:

> The theoretical underpinnings for today's far right originated at the time of the French Revolution in the creation of the myth of an "international Jewish conspiracy." Evolving and expanding over the years, this myth worked its way through Europe in the early twentieth century, and was popularized in America during the 1920s, when fear and antagonism towards immigrants and naturalized aliens was at its height. Automobile tycoon Henry Ford was one of the first and most influential promulgators of the doctrine of an international Jewish conspiracy; and the idea was taken up by the burgeoning Ku Klux Klan, and added to its already busy agenda of anti-black and anti-Catholic terror.[22]

Although the myth, which began in 1797, weaves its way through a maze of casuistry and intrigue, focusing especially upon the role of secret societies in the decline of public morality which led to the French Revolution, Jewish people first became implicated in the myth in 1806, when they were accused of accumulating wealth and influence for the purpose of controlling the world. The major outlines of this myth were written down in a document called the "Protocols of the Meetings of the Learned Elders of Zion." In it, Jewish people were accused of destablizing the social order, starting wars for their own economic gain, creating huge monopolies, and inappropriately influencing national governments. In a sinister document called "The Rabbi's Speech," published throughout Europe, the anonymous author "described how once every hundred years, the reigning elders of the twelve tribes of Israel gathered around the grave of the most senior rabbi and issued reports on the progress of the grand plot to enslave the gentiles and take over the world."[23] In the modern era, the myth took root in the United States with the help of industrialist Henry Ford. Ford capitalized on the fears and insecurities of Americans during the 1920s and published a series of articles based on the "Protocols" in his newspaper, the *Dearborn Independent*.[24] The *Independent* fanned the flames of hatred by blaming international warfare on Jews, by accusing Jews of infiltrating U.S. government at the highest levels, and by enriching themselves at the expense of others. Ford added to these traditional elements of the conspiracy theory some new claims which spoke to the evolution of popular culture in the United States. Jewish people were accused of controlling the theater and entertainment industries, of introducing American youth to "popular music" with its sensual and immoral overtones, of promoting alcoholism, of corrupting the all-American sport of baseball, and of introducing female mud wrestling to the American public.[25] In essence, the myth of the international Jewish conspiracy was employed to explain the bewildering changes in economics, culture, and global politics experienced by a people who longed for simpler days. The U.S. government was subsequently referred to by white supremacists as the "Zionist Occupation Government," and Jewish people were referred to as "demon Jews" or "Satan's offspring."

The theoretical underpinnings of white supremacist hatred of African Americans was less complex, even if the hatred itself was perhaps more severe. The physical color of black people made them easily identifiable targets, thus there was no need for a conspiracy theory to justify their oppression. From the same Enlightenment era that gave rise to the myth of the Jewish conspiracy came the scientific and religious theories of racial inferiority that focused on black people. The history of color symbolism in the West, and its confluence with powerful religious tropes of good and evil, purity and taint, lent credence to the idea that African Americans were lower on the evolutionary scale than people of European descent. There were two major tenets in the canopy of racism against black people. First, the white race had to be protected against the taint of the black presence. Hence, complete separation was necessary. Second, the supposedly unbridled and animalistic sex drive of African Americans was the main conduit of their corrupting influence. In a sense, white supremacists drew on the distinctly Puritan notion of the relationship between sex, sin, and blackness to erect a scaffold upon which African Americans could be lynched both literally and figuratively. In sum, one could say that the rise of white supremacy in the United States was a particularly abhorrent manifestation of the white revolt against that sea-change in American life which we now refer to as modernism.

The ideological buttress for white supremacy is a pseudo-theology called Christian Identity. This ideology is embraced by many fundamentalist but less overtly racist religious communities such as the Church of Israel, the Gospel of Christ Kingdom Church, and the World Wide Church of God, among others.[26] But it also provides the foundation for the vast majority of white supremacist groups in the United States today. The origins of Christian Identity are difficult to locate. Some scholars trace its origins to the 1840 publication of Scotsman John Wilson's *Our Israelitish Origin*.[27] Others claim that it was founded by the Englishman, Edward Hine, in his 1871 book, *Identification of the British Nation with Lost Israel*. The common element in both instances was the search for the lost tribes of Israel. The conclusion of both books provided the basis for the doctrine of Christian Identity:

> The crux of the doctrine is that European Jews are not descended from ancient Hebrew stock at all but from Khazars, residents of a warlike nation of southern Russia who converted to Judaism in the eighth or ninth century. They cannot claim lineage from Abraham, Isaac, and Jacob and are not the covenant people, according to Identity's genealogists. On the contrary, today's Nordic-Anglo-Saxon-Teuton whites are the descendants of the lost tribes of the Biblical Israelites, making white Christians the true people of the covenant. To support this, Hine reinterpreted the book of Genesis with a "two seed theory." Eve was seduced by the serpent and bore a son by him, Cain, who slew his broth-

er Abel. After that Adam, the first white man, passed on his seed to another son, Seth, who became the father of the white race, God's Chosen People. Cain's descendants, Identity says, are the Jews. They literally are the seed of Satan. Other races, or "mud people" to racists, descend from others cursed by God.[28]

British Israelism, as it came to be known, was imported to Canada and the United States during the first decades of the twentieth century. It spilled over the Canadian border from Vancouver, British Columbia, into the states of Washington and Oregon. It also found its way into the eastern United States from the eastern Canadian provinces into the state of Maine. An odd twist in the development of Christian Identity was the fact that some Identity believers came to regard Native Americans as the true Aryan people. "The fascination with Native Americans is also a longstanding Klan preoccupation: many Klansmen try to trace their heritage back through the blue eyes and finely chiseled features of certain American Indian tribes, to the Celts, and, finally, to the lost tribes of Israel."[29] In the context of contemporary U.S. political discourse:

> Identity theory teaches that the U.S. is God's promised land and modern Israel a hoax. British followers of Identity are starkly anti-Semitic, but it was the American Identity theologians who added the ingeniously gnostic racist twist known as the "two seed" theory. They hold that the non-white races are "pre-Adamic"—that is, part of the creation finished *before* God created Adam and Eve. In his wisdom, they say, God fashioned the subhuman nonwhites and sent them to live outside the Garden of Eden before the Fall. When Eve broke God's original commandment, she was implanted with two seeds. From Adam's seed sprang Abel and the white race. From the serpent Satan's seed came the lazy, wicked Cain. Angered, God cast Adam, Eve, and the serpent out of the Garden of Eden and decreed eternal racial conflict. Cain killed Abel, then ran off into the jungle to join the pre-Adamic nonwhites. . . . Identity theology provides both a religious base for racism and anti-Semitism, and an ideological rationale for violence against minorities and their white allies.[30]

With its two-seed theory, originated perhaps by Hine and developed by his successors, Identity theology became a viable alternative for disaffected fundamentalists. These fundamentalists gave to Identity theology a racist cast directed not only toward Jews but primarily toward African Americans. Identity theology gave refuge to fundamentalists who could not understand the support given to the state of Israel by many of their more well known preachers. It is at this point—because many of the early U.S. Identity proponents were former Christian fundamentalists—that the coupling of Identity theory and Christian Dispensationalism resulted in a distinctive hybrid form.

Identity theory explains reality in basically dualistic terms. God is in conflict with the devil. The forces of light, goodness, chastity, cleanliness, and purity are locked in battle against the forces of evil, lewdness, stain, and defilement. Unlike traditional formal explanations of this dualism, however, Identity theory does not teach that this struggle goes on in every human being but that it goes on *among* different groups of people. This does not mean, however, that the tendency to assign the label of the "evil ones" to other groups of people is absent in traditional Christian theological thought. There are too many examples of the dehumanization of other human beings in the name of "the church" for that. The point here is that in Identity theory, the notion of the inner struggle of the human being is entirely absent. Thus, racist Identity followers can refer to African Americans and others as "human rodents," "pests," "germs," "viruses," and "bacteria." Certainly, questionable exegesis of the Bible is required to support the theological infrastructure of Identity theory; however, an ironic twist is that much of the support for this racist and anti-Semitic view comes from certain Rabbinical texts in which the humanity of black people is called into question.[31] The apocryphal *First Book of Enoch* describes the origins of social pathology in a story in which the fallen angels of heaven succumb to their lust for earthly maidens, cohabitate with them and produce a race of black mutant devils.[32] What the Identity theologians grasped from their twisted reading of the Bible is an emphasis on racial hygiene and the personification of evil in "the other." This racial purity is symbolized by the ability to blush, to have "blood in the face."

Much of the compelling force of Identity theory is the result of its emphasis on an apocalyptic eschatology. In it the focus on Armageddon reemerges:

> Christian Identity followers tend to think in apocalyptic terms. Many believe that the era of the beast is fast approaching; some think the field of Armageddon is in Nebraska or Kansas. Some see in our current system of banking and commerce the very signs foretold in the Book of Revelation. To many on the fringe, this trend represents the dreaded mark of the beast, without which in Apostle John's nightmarish vision, "no one could get a job or even buy in any store" (Rev. 13:17).[33]

In this view, history will end, not in the nuclear nightmare that haunts much of the postmodern consciousness but in a cultural holocaust. To preserve the chosen white saints of God, strict separation of the races is required. Thus, in one elaborate scheme, the United States is divided into separate racial homelands. Navahona and Alta California, both in the southwestern portion of the United States, are the names of the regions set aside for Native Americans and Mexican Americans, respectively. East Mongolia, in the Hawaiian Islands, and New Cuba, in the city of Miami, Florida, are the homelands of Asian Americans and Cuban Americans, respectively. West Israel is located in Long Island and Manhattan; Minoria, set aside for Puerto Ricans, Italians, and Greeks, takes up the remainder of New York City. Francia, in northern New England, is the new home of the French-Canadian community in the United States; and New Africa, the reserve for people of African descent, is located in the southeastern portion of the country. Some, but not all, white supremacists groups, identify a "white bastion" located in the area that is now the states of Washington, Oregon, Montana, Wyoming, and Idaho.[34] This dividing of the land completes the eschatological circle of white supremacy in which people with different histories—that is, who occupy different locations on the time continuum—are also people of separate lands—that is, who occupy different locations on the space continuum. Ironically, rather than a hopeful eschatology, what one finds in the ideological infrastructure of white supremacist dogma is a fatalistic resignation in which the United States—once claimed to be the Promised Land—is divided up among warring factions.

Reexamining Eschatology

Our focus is the relationship between the idea of eschatology or hope in mainline Christian thought and the fundamental vision of white supremacist groups in the United States. We have briefly reviewed the notion of eschatology in Christian theology, and the theological roots of white supremacy. We have discussed the ways in which Christian thought in the United States is related to the vision of white supremacy. It remains to be seen, in light of that relation, how Christian notions of eschatology might be revised. The eschatological dimensions of white supremacy suggests at least three concepts which require reexamination.

The first concept is the meaning of history and hope. One of the central affirmations of the Christian faith is that there is a definite relationship between the history and hope of a people. When the people of Israel left Egypt, they remembered the promise extracted from them by Joseph, who asked that they take his bones with them (Exod. 13:18-

19). The hope of Israel, which lay in land that God had promised to them, could never be separated from their history of enslavement, degradation, and dislocation in Egypt. The prophets constantly reminded a stiff-necked, and often forgetful, people that the God who guaranteed their future was the same God who brought them out of the house of bondage (Jer. 2:5-6; Ezek. 20:9-10). Jesus' ministry, too, rested on the authority of Israel's God. This authority was mediated through, though not limited to, the history and tradition of Israel. The hope for humanity, as embodied in Jesus himself, was inseparable from what God had done in the history of Israel.

One of the dimensions of white supremacist thought which presents itself clearly in relation to eschatology, is that many of its adherents see themselves as a people without a history. Among many white supremacists there is a kind of *cultural amnesia* in which race is elevated to the level of supreme norm, while ethnicity is denied. It is curious that white supremacists completely ignore their own European ethnicity and elect to establish their identity by adopting the label "white" to describe themselves. Whiteness, like blackness for that matter, is a North American trope born out of the racial polarization endemic to the society. It speaks to one's political, rather than cultural, location.[35] The national myth which claims that all who come to U.S. shores are enjoined to leave their cultural particularity behind them is part of the explanation of this phenomenon. The normative cultural context of the United States is one in which everyone, except those whose lineage goes back to the *Mayflower*, is encouraged to dehistoricize themselves and to blend, if possible, into the normative culture. Most followers of white supremacy share with the cultural powerholders in society only skin color—race not ethnicity. With no cultural history to draw upon, they simply invented a racial history.

Besides cultural amnesia, white supremacist writings betray a kind of *political fatalism.* That is, a people without a sense of a cultural history will also be a people without political hope. In spite of the bravado and posturing of many leaders of the white supremacist movement, a definite fatalism tinges their proclamations. Within their revolutionary rhetoric is none of the optimism one would expect of persons who are absolutely certain of the rightness of their cause. Very little concrete detail is given in descriptions of the future, beyond the establishment of a "Miracle Whip Kultur," in which the white race is dominant. The lack of political substance in the vision of white supremacists is perhaps what allows them to attract a variety of followers, including those anarchists who have lost all faith in the political possibilities for community in the postmodern world. In light of these considerations, it is incumbent upon the Christian church to emphasize that without a common history, there can be no common hope. Each person must be able to find his or her place in the history of humanity told in the biblical witness, and the church is where that place should be affirmed and celebrated. Moreover, it is through the retelling of our histories and the sharing of our hopes that true community is created.

The second eschatological concept that requires revision is the relationship between creation and consummation. In a sense, this concept is analogous to that of history and hope, but on a cosmic scale. It deals with the origins and destiny of the created order. The symmetry of the biblical witness suggests a significant relationship between the emphases found in the creation accounts and those encountered in the narrative of the consummation of history. The creation accounts in the Book of Genesis are usually cited as mythopoetic expressions of the beginning of all that is. White supremacists have fastened on that aspect of the creation narratives which deals with the origin of evil, sin, and human alienation. Much of the ideological justification for their racist views is founded on a twisted, but not uncommon, interpretation of the temptation of Adam and Eve, and their eventual expulsion from the Garden of Eden. As noted above, this interpretation justifies the separation of the races which grew out of human strife.

The conflicts that initiated in the creation accounts find their resolution in the biblical accounts of the consummation of history. Thus, the Book of Revelation provides, for white supremacists, an account of rapture, tribulation, suffering, and conflict that will issue forth in a pure white race. In essence, if the history of the world originates with human strife, it will end with human strife. The relationship between creation and consummation in Christian theology in the North American context needs to be revised in light of the challenge of white supremacist interpretations. Certainly, violence is part of the creation narrative, and the realignment of the social order is part of the consummation narrative. The question is whether these are the central interpretive foci for creation and consummation. The creation narratives are misunderstood if they are taken to be accounts of the origins of human existence. Biblical scholars have agreed that the earliest collective memory of Israel centers on the Exodus. The Exodus account is actually more than the story of a mass escape from bondage. Its focus is the creation of community. It is in this context that God tells God's people, "I will take you who were no people and make you my people" (Exod. 6:7). The peoplehood of Israel is established by God's mighty acts on their behalf. Further, this community is not founded on the notion of racial purity or homogeneity.[36] This community is made up of persons whose "Mother was a Hittite, and whose father was a Amorite (Ezek. 16:45). Likewise, the Book of Revelation is not primarily concerned with the destruction of the created order but with its redemption. Its final goal is overcoming sin and alienation, and establishing the beloved community. As the writer of Revelation surveyed the horizon of human history, he saw beyond the pain and suffering which his community was undergoing at that moment and glimpsed "a new heaven, and a new earth." He saw a "new Jerusalem," a new community, and its citizens found their identity firmly inscribed in "the Book of Life."

The third concept in Christian eschatology which requires revision in light of the establishment of community is that of apocalypse and judgment. In white supremacist rhetoric, apocalyptic language is the vehicle for the horror that results when the people of God come face to face with God's judgment. Although this language has often been used to instill fear in the hearts of neophyte Christians, this is not the central role of apocalyptic language in biblical discourse. The apocalyptic images found in the Book of Daniel, for example, do certainly address the impending judgment of the Babylonian Empire, but their primary purpose is to reveal the creation of community in exile. In the context of wars for territorial and ethnic conquest between Greece and Persia, the point of Daniel's vision of death and overthrow is that true community begins in the righteousness of God (Dan. 12:1-4). Likewise, the Book of Revelation speaks to the divine redemption of all that is, employing dramatic images of God's rectification of all that humanity has set askew.

The essence of this redemption is the establishment of the beloved community. The writer of Revelation first sees the beloved community as composed of the 144,000 who bear the seal of God upon their foreheads (Rev. 7:3). But that number cannot express the radical inclusivity of the community of the redeemed, because the writer then sees "a great multitude which no one could number, from every nation, from all tribes and peoples and tongues . . ." (Rev. 7:9).

The word *apocalypse* means disclosure. The primary content of Christian apocalyptic is not disaster or condemnation, but the revelation of the coming community of God. Beyond "the terrible beast" and the "lake of fire," there is the vision of a restored community in which the original harmony among persons and nature is affirmed. The writer of Revelation shares with the reader a vision which recalls the

Garden of Eden. "Then he showed me the river of the water of life, bright as crystal, flowing from the throne of God and of the Lamb through the middle of the street of the city: also, on either side of the river, the tree of life with its twelve kinds of fruit, yielding its fruit each month; and the leaves of the tree were for the healing of the nations" (Rev. 22:1).

Toward the Beloved Community

What will it take to make the beloved community—one which truly values human diversity—a reality? The poignant story of a former white supremacist suggests that, at the very least, the civic virtues of solidarity and neighborliness are required. In 1979 Greg Withrow founded the White Student Union, later called "the Aryan Youth Movement," at American River College in Sacramento, California. In 1987, Withrow fell in love and, influenced by his companion, publicly rejected his racist views. Shortly thereafter, a group of his former colleagues attacked and brutally beat him. Calling him a "traitor," they nailed his hands to a crossbeam, slashed him with a knife, and left him for dead (in the parking lot of K-Mart, no less!). He regained consciousness and, with the crossbeam still on his back, hobbled down the street seeking assistance. He appealed to a white woman who simply turned away. A white couple did likewise. But a black couple coming out of a nightclub came to his aid. They took the gag from his mouth and called the police. Reflecting on this event, Withrow observed, "I want people to see that this is what I get because this is what I created. What goes around comes around."[37] Within this story, with its remarkable allusions to the Crucifixion and the parable of the Good Samaritan, are the foundations of the beloved community that ought to be central to the proclamation and praxis of the churches in these days of racial tension and conflict.

Historically, Christian communities have been engaged in the practices of building social structures that fit somewhere on the continuum between paradise and the apocalypse. Yet the ideologies that lie behind these practices are often inimical to the formation of loving communities. It is imperative that churches recover the deep propensity for self-critique. This self-critique will plunge the churches directly into the struggles and ambiguities of its host cultures. In her book *The Politics of God*, Kathryn Tanner describes two types of cultures. Customary cultures, as she describes them, are those in which social transformations are the results of "unreflective habits," while reflective cultures are those in which social transformations are "promoted by reflection on principles or standards of procedure, and in that way produce a self-critical culture."[38] In the context of the United States, both types of culture are present. Churches, however, have rarely engaged in the sustained reflection necessary to develop a consistent self-critique. Rather than leading the movement toward justice, therefore, churches have too often limped along into the future in an unreflective response to general social change.

The beloved community, as I understand it, is a community with a highly developed and consistent culture of self-critique. The story cited above suggests that there are at least three dimensions to this self-critique. First, this self-critique makes confession possible. Withrow was able to confess his transgressions because he was loved. It was not simply romantic love but a love that also shattered his allegiance to oppressive forces. Second, this self-critique made it possible to see the other in a different light. Here, the African American couple who rescued him were able to see Withrow as another suffering human being who stood in need of assistance. Third, Withrow was able to discern, within the total context of his experience, the meaning of his own suffering in relation to that which he had inflicted upon others.

The beloved community in the United States will recognize the ambiguity that surrounds all of its practices. That is, it is always susceptible to sin. This is what Martin Luther King Jr. meant when he stated, "The American people are infected with racism—that is the peril. Paradoxically, they are also infected with democratic ideals—that is the hope."[39] This means that both the internal and external practices of the churches will be guided by a commitment to justice, realizing that imperfect justice is redeemed by love. It can certainly be argued that not every Christian community occupies that same moral ground or, therefore, possesses the same propensity toward this self-critique. The point, however, is that the possibility for self-critique is in some measure present in every Christian community.

To participate in the up-building of the beloved community means that we must be able to share the sufferings of another, and we must be willing to answer the question, "Who is my neighbor?" with genuine acts of compassion. Perhaps then, out of a history of pain, enmity, and hostility, we can grasp what Vincent Harding has called "one final, soaring hope."[40]

5 Spiritual Renewal and Social Transformation

The hand of the Lord was upon me, and he brought me out by the Spirit of the Lord, and set me down in the midst of the valley; and it was full of bones. And he led me round among them; and behold, there were very many upon the valley; and lo, they were very dry. And he said to me, "Son of man, can these bones live?"
—Ezekiel 37:1-3

One of the ironies in Western societies at the end of the second millennium is the coincidence of two deeply felt needs. Out of the vacuity of a consumerist and materialistic culture has emerged, from a surprising variety of contexts, a public longing for spiritual renewal. This widespread and often inchoate dissatisfaction with bureaucratic ratiocination and with the disjunction of knowledge from morality, science from art, fact from feeling is most clearly seen in the rejection of the extremes of modernism and the emergence of the postmodern mood.[1] The second deeply felt need is related to the challenges to community brought on by the changing shapes of many Western societies. The onset of ethnic conflicts and persistent religious warfare have amply illustrated our deep frustration in the search for what Howard Thurman called "common ground." We are aware, in some profound sense, that we are in need of a social conversion. We know that we need some kind of social transformation.

The irony of our times is that these two powerfully felt needs are rarely seen as related to one another. That is, we fail to connect our desire for spiritual renewal to our need for social transformation. In one sense, this failure is related to the longstanding Western dualism which divides our existence into distinct spiritual and material dimensions. The provocative image of the valley of dry bones found in the prophecy of Ezekiel is notable because it reminds us that the reclamation of a wholistic social and material existence is inseparable from the revival of our individual spiritual lives. In this story the prophet is shown an image of a society that has been stripped of its connective tissue and its life force. Even when the bones have been reassembled, it is not until the life force from God has been restored that an authentic spiritual and social existence is possible again. This suggests that, in spite of all of our attempts to shape society in ways that are more just and loving, the results will be sterile structures until the spirit of God is present. Because this association has been too often ignored, religious and political authority has been eclipsed and both our sacred and secular rituals have become empty. The question which shapes this chapter is: How can we reconceptualize the relationship between spiritual renewal and social transformation so that we might be whole again? The question itself is a wide river with dozens of tributaries. The aim of this chapter is to explore one of those streams. Its course will take us from a consideration of the roots of African American spirituality to a preliminary suggestion regarding contemporary resources for spiritual renewal and social transformation.

Spirituality and Social Transformation

Spirituality is sometimes associated with certain disciplines of prayer and reflection. Yet spirituality is more basic than this. It refers to the heart of religion as the quest for communion with God as God is known both within and outside of ourselves. Spirituality or spiritualities are funded by our understanding of the divine spirit and the human spirit. Since the emergence of various forms of liberation theology, corresponding spiritualities have often been related to the political order. One writer notes that

> Liberation spirituality is, therefore, a political spirituality—this point should not be concealed—and it is concerned and involved with material things like bread, clothing, health, and shelter. In this sense liberation spirituality is "materialistic." However, it is there in these material things

that this spirituality primarily encounters Jesus, the Jesus who is the person in need. . . . With one stroke, liberation spirituality unites love for God and love for neighbor, this life and the next, the "material" world and the "spiritual" world.[2]

Is this form of spirituality germane to the social transformation we need? It is true that spirituality is related to politics. But the political realm is only one aspect of human existence. In essence, politics are simply the power struggles that occur as a society seeks to align and realign itself in its attempt to manage social transitions that have already begun or taken place. In addition, political spiritualities are sometimes prone to focus on providing solace within or retreat from actual social change. Thus, even "political spiritualities" can be ascetic. So the issue is more complex and comprehensive than politics. A spirituality that promises to reorient us in these days must engage and understand the character of and the deep currents within the massive social changes now affecting contemporary societies.

One of the curious phenomena of our times is the emergence of spiritualities that are not demonstrably connected with any of the historical Christian communities. While some Christian thinkers are inclined to dismiss these contemporary spiritual quests as the misguided wanderings of Generation X or the unchurched, it is quite possible that these movements are related to the massive social changes that have occurred and continue to occur in this century. The speculations of futurists like Alvin Toffler and others have gained a wide reading because they attempt to set in a broader explanatory matrix the transformations which confront us today. An example is Peter Drucker's provocative essay, "The Age of Social Transformation." Drucker argues that "no century in recorded history has experienced so many social transformations and such radical ones as the twentieth century."[3] Drucker identifies three major paradigms that have shaped life particularly in the developed free-market nations and that have had tremendous impact on the fates of other countries as well. The social transformations that have demolished one paradigm and fueled the emergence of the next have been remarkable because they have—unlike the social transformations of prior centuries—been subtle and nonviolent.

Far smaller and far slower social changes in earlier periods triggered civil wars, rebellions, and violent intellectual and spiritual crises. The extreme social transformations of this century have caused hardly any stir. They have proceeded with a minimum of friction, with a minimum of upheavals, and, indeed, with a minimum of attention from scholars, politicians, the press, and the public.[4]

Drucker acknowledges that the twentieth century has been a violent one, with more than its share of wars, mass killings, genocidal campaigns, and the like. Yet the fact is that these events were not related to any significant social transformations. "Hitler, Stalin, and Mao, the three evil geniuses of this century, destroyed. They created nothing."[5] The major shifts of this century involved the transformation of the political economy from an agricultural economy, to an industrial economy, to an economy based on knowledge.

At the opening of the twentieth century the largest single group in every country in the world were farmers. Within developed countries, the second largest group were live-in servants. Within a very short period of time, however, the percentage of the populations engaged in farm work shrank dramatically, and live-in servants as a group have almost disappeared completely. At the end of the twentieth century "productive farmers make up . . . less than two percent of the workforce . . . [and] live-in domestic servants scarcely exist in developed countries."[6] This tremendous social transformation took place without upheaval because of the opportunities created by the industrial revolution. The employment created by industry was unique in that so-called blue-collar workers found themselves in a position to affect the conditions of employment, wages and benefits, and even political elections. The rise of labor unions assured that industrial laborers acquired an unprecedented social status and middle-class incomes. Farmers and domestic servants left their former positions in large numbers to take advantage of a higher standard of living, more predictable working conditions, and the opportunity to advance in social status. Still, within one lifetime the fortunes of blue-collar workers have risen and fallen. "No class in history has ever risen faster than the blue collar worker. And no class in history has ever fallen faster."[7] While industrial workers enjoyed benefits that prior groups of workers never had—pensions, paid vacations, overtime pay, a five-day regular work week, health insurance—by the last decade of the twentieth century their power had waned considerably. The blue-collar worker has fallen as a class but has not disappeared. This shift in fortunes is the result of a second massive social change. This change, too, has occurred without physical violence.

The latter part of the twentieth century has witnessed the emergence of the "knowledge society" and the rise of the "knowledge worker." In this third paradigm, knowledge is capital. In the "knowledge society,"

> Knowledge has become the key resource, for a nation's military strength as well as for its economic strength. And this knowledge can be acquired only through schooling. It is not tied to any country. It is portable. It can be created everywhere, fast and cheaply. Finally, it is by definition changing. Knowledge as the key resource is fundamentally different from the traditional key resources of the economist—land, labor, and even capital.[8]

This transformation differs significantly from that which ushered in the industrial age. The knowledge age does not offer the same opportunities for the displaced industrial worker. "The great majority of the new jobs require qualifications the industrial worker does not possess and is poorly equipped to acquire. They require a good deal of formal education and the ability to acquire and to apply theoretical and analytical knowledge."[9] The knowledge worker will have a kind of social influence not enjoyed by his or her industrial predecessors. The productivity of knowledge workers will be determined by what they know rather than the efficiency of their tools, machinery, or their possession of material capital. "Education will become the center of the knowledge society, and the school its key institution."[10] This social transformation will also have a significant affect on major institutions like our family, the town, and even the notion of a neighborhood. Two major aspects of this latter social transformation which are significant for the purposes. The first is the declining influence of economic interests. A politics based on economic interests can no longer provide a structural basis for civil society, says Drucker:

> Increasingly, politics is not about "who gets what, when, how" but about values, each of them considered to be an absolute. Politics is about the right to life of the embryo in the womb as against the right of a woman to control her own body and to abort an embryo. It is about the environment. It is about gaining equality for groups alleged to be oppressed and discriminated against. None of these issues is economic. All are fundamentally moral. Economic interests can be compromised, which is the great strength of basing politics on economic interests. [With values, however,] no compromise is possible.[11]

The emergence of the knowledge society, in Drucker's view, promises social benefits and moral challenges. The second major aspect of this social transformation which is important for this essay is the persistence of the "Negro Problem." Drucker notes that the shift from an industrial society to a knowledge society

> has aggravated America's oldest and least tractable problem: the position of blacks. In the fifty years since the Second World War the economic position of African Americans in America has improved faster than that of any other group in American social history. . . . Since the Second World War more and more blacks have moved into blue-collar unionized mass-production industry—that is, into jobs paying middle-class and upper-middle-class wages while requiring neither education nor skill. These are precisely the jobs, however, that are disappearing the fastest. What is amazing is not that so many blacks did not acquire an education but that so many did.[12]

In essence, the emergence of this new knowledge society brings with it two problems, one moral, religious, and perhaps even theological, and the other social. Yet the coincidence of these problems—the problem of finding a moral center in a society where the basis is shifting, and the "Negro Problem"—suggests that a spirituality which has promise in this emerging society must embrace both its moral and social aspects.

African Americans have been both swept up and left behind by the massive social transformations of the twentieth century. In the nineteenth and early twentieth centuries, African Americans were either slaves or primarily sharecroppers and thus did not share in the bounty available in the heyday of agricultural society. In the middle of the twentieth century, African Americans gained entry into the industrial order just as it was declining. The emergence of the knowledge society will shape our moral dilemmas in new ways and give rise to new manifestations of the "Negro Problem." It may be fairly stated that the fundamental moral dilemmas of our time will continue to find paradigmatic expression in the social problems of black people. It may also be fairly stated that the route to authentic spiritual renewal in our day will lead through the folkways of people of African descent.

African Spirituality

In his important book, *The Spirituality of African Peoples*, Peter J. Paris examines the distinctive features of African spirituality both on the African continent and in the diaspora. He defines spirituality as "the animating and integrative power that constitutes the principal frame of meaning for individual and collective experiences. Metaphorically, the spirituality of a people is synonymous with the soul of a people: the integrating center of their power and meaning."[13] Paris argues that African spirituality is always an embodied spirituality, fully connected with the dynamic—and I would add *social*—movement of life. "On the one hand, the goal of that movement is the struggle for survival while, on the other hand, it is the union of those forces of life that have the power either to threaten and destroy life on the one hand, or to preserve and enhance it, on the other hand."[14] A central feature of African spirituality is its hospitality, as seen in its tolerance of other religious traditions.

African spirituality has survived the transition to the New World in ways that are clearly recognizable. The point here is not to verify that certain African cultural traditions have endured through the experience to slavery and dislocation. The point is to understand how people of African descent have drawn on their indigenous resources in creative ways to make life more liveable. In a fascinating book, *Flash of the Spirit*, Robert Farris Thompson argues that the common and unifying feature of African art and philosophy is its focus on the spirit. This spirit finds expression in song, dance, and the ritual practices that give order and meaning to life. "Listening to rock, jazz, blues, reggae, salsa, samba, bossa nova, juju, highlife, and mambo, one might conclude that much of the popular music of the world is informed by the flash of the spirit of a certain people specially armed with improvisatory drive and brilliance."[15] This spirit is associated with life and is often symbolized by a tree. Thompson points out that the tree is used throughout the African diaspora to decorate graves as a sign representing spiritual mediation. "In other words, the tree stands sentinel above the grave as the immortal presence of the spirit, an image that graces countless Afro-American burials . . . where stone and tree represent together the departed person."[16] *Spirit* in African traditions is not only the essence of life, it refers to the quality of life. The "quality of life" aspect of the spirit in African traditions is seen in the primacy of healing in indigenous spirituality. The healing function of the spirit is mediated through the material world. Natural objects, properly used, can be agents of healing and wholeness. This is the reason that the term "medicine" takes on a much broader meaning than is ordinarily the case. In African spirituality, medicine is more than a substance which has a pharmaceutical function related to the altering of the chemical balances in the body. In African spirituality, medicines have two major religious functions. They are either *spirit-embodying* medicines or *spirit-directing* medicines. "Spirit-embodying materials include cemetery earth—considered at one with the spirit of a buried person."[17] Spirit-embodying materials or medicines are believed to contain the vital life force necessary for human existence. Spirit-directing medicines include such materials as seeds, stones, herbs, or sticks and provide spiritual instruction. In essence, spirit-directing medicines provide guidance in the affairs of life, while spirit-embodying medicines brings people into contact with the source of the sustenance of life.[18] The function of medicines in African spirituality points to the central feature of that spirituality. "African spirituality is based on this centrality of human beings presently living in the concrete circumstances of life this side of the grave. . . . The central concern is how to make sense of this life and ensure that it is meaningful, harmonious, good, and worth living."[19] In addition, African spirituality is concerned with the issues of survival in hostile circumstances. This is why the prayers and petitions of traditional African religions focus on the things which are basic to the survival of the community. This survival is dependent upon two fundamental needs and the assistance of the community in meeting them:

> On the one hand, people ask for what they need to survive and live well, and on the other they ask to be protected from evil. . . . Two elements, then, animate African spirituality: first, the consciousness that individuals and the community are committed to an ever-present struggle against menacing evil if life is to be worth living; and secondly, that in this struggle the decisive key is the availability of assistance from the invisible. Furthermore, there is the conviction that this struggle is not pursued by individuals alone in isolation, but that it is in and through the community that the fight can be carried on effectively. African spirituality relies on the spirit of community, on cooperation rather than open competition, on sharing and redistribution, rather than on accumulation or individualistic hoarding.[20]

In its nascent state African spirituality manifested a wholistic approach to life and its challenges. But there is a temptation to see African spirituality in romantic and unrealistic terms. The power and efficacy of any spirituality are evident in its ability to assist its community in meeting the demands of a constantly changing world. African theologian Patrick Kalilombe observes that

> The African way of life, which is the background against which spirituality needs to be examined, is not something static. Over the centuries, African societies have been in constant transformation, mainly due to interactions with the outside, but also due to changing conditions of life,

new needs, development of ideas, and modification of techniques and values. . . . If, indeed, spirituality is an aspect of human culture, it can only be discovered authentically where people's actual way of life is going on. And so, African spirituality today should be examined within the complexity of present culture change, and not in some romantic and artificial reconstruction of traditional life that is no more really there.[21]

African spirituality is important because of the way that is has functioned and adapted itself to tremendous social transformations. These transformations have altered life in African communities at a variety of levels and have all been associated, in one way or another, with the institution of the Atlantic slave trade and the subsequent processes of colonialism. Colonialism, in its political, economic, and cultural forms, brought powerful changes to indigenous patterns of existence, exchange, and expression. Its major impact, however, was the introduction of an alternative spirituality. Kalilombe argues that

the key to a proper understanding of what is going on is to realize that contact with the outside has introduced a new, alternative spirituality based on a worldview quite different from the traditional one and governed by a different set of values and priorities. This new spirituality is humanly more powerful and imposing. It promises attractive, immediate, and palpable results and has the capacity to validate these promises by offering samples of success that are hard to ignore or pass by. Central to this spirituality is the supremacy of the value of acquiring, possessing, multiplying, and enjoying material goods by individuals.[22]

Besides the spirituality of a imperial and materialistic culture, colonialism also brought with it the spirituality of Western Christianity. While in many ways the spirituality of Western Christianity resisted modern materialism and condemned traditional African culture, Africans found that resistance to be shallow and that condemnation to be unfounded. That is, Western Christian spirituality was too closely aligned with the interests of colonialism, and Christian spirituality stripped of its Western bias had much in common with traditional African spirituality. Nonetheless, it was only in the context of a profound and ongoing social transformation that the true efficacy of African spirituality could be assessed.

As tens of millions of Africans were taken into slavery, many relied upon their spirituality to assist them in their struggle for freedom and wholeness. George Cummings notes that the slaves' invocation of the Spirit "entailed the affirmation of independence and selfhood; sustained hope for freedom as embodied in their prayer life; served as the basis of love within the slave community; and even assisted slaves in their desire to escape to freedom."[23] Slave spirituality involved survival of the community and meeting its basic needs. Moreover, this spirituality involved, and in some instances became synonymous with, creativity in the face of racial oppression. The spirit was the power to adapt to changing social circumstances but also the power to change those circumstances themselves. In this sense slave spirituality was intimately connected with both personal responses to change, and with social transformation itself.

African Spirituality and the Church

African spirituality carried within it the capacity to shape personal responses to significant social changes and to fuel the effort to transform society itself. As African Christian churches were formed they struggled to incorporate this spirituality. For reasons both numerous and complex, however, the socially radical function of spirituality could not be accommodated to the structure and self-perception of these emergent ecclesial communities.[24] Therefore those African and African American churches that emphasized the Holy Spirit tended to focus on the role of the spirit in assisting their members in shaping their personal responses to social change for the purposes of survival.

One example of this phenomenon is the story of the the Independent Holy Spirit Churches founded in the Eastern regions of the African continent around the beginning of the twentieth century. These Holy Spirit churches grew initially out of the African mission effort of the Society of Friends. In 1927 one of the missionary preachers delivered a sermon that had unexpected results:

> In September 1927 there was a yearly meeting of the Friends Africa Mission at Kaimosa. Arthur Chilson, the missionary in charge of the meeting, decided to deliver the message of Pentecost to the people assembled there. He told them that to be a true Christian required baptism with the Holy Spirit and that to receive this baptism it was necessary to confess all one's sins openly and to pray for forgiveness. His message strongly affected his listeners. They knelt down, they confessed and asked God to forgive their sins. When this had been going on for some time, Arthur Chilson stood up and lifted his hands over the heads of the congregation. He prayed that they might receive the baptism with the Holy Spirit. The meeting was now seized by the Spirit. People were crying, everything was shaking, and many began to speak in tongues. To show them

the biblical authority for what they had just experienced, Chilson read Acts 2:1-4.[25]

This account—which has striking similarities to those of the Azusa Street movement, which gave birth to the Pentecostal movement in the United States—describes a free and unfettered irruption of the Holy Spirit. The outpouring, however, unmasked significant theological differences between the Society of Friends and their African converts around the meaning of the Holy Spirit. The African converts insisted that the baptism of the Holy Spirit required speaking in tongues and publicly confessing one's sins. These acts were percieved as socially unacceptable as well as theologically suspect by the Society of Friends, whose demeanor in worship and whose theology were more subdued. The Society of Friends missionaries insisted that the Africans cease these activities. The resulting tensions are evident in the following report:

> When in 1929 the Friends' elders had not suceeded in threatening the people from Bukoyani and Muhanda into giving up their open confessions and their belief in the outpouring of the Holy Spirit, they called them in front of their committee. Here they were told that the spirit they had was a bad one, and that if they would not give up their confessions and their shouting and speaking in tongues, they would be expelled from the Friends Africa Mission. Jacob Bukulu now stood up as the spokesman of the Holy Spirit people. He answered the elders that if the spirit which had seized them had been a bad one it would not have revealed all people's sins, and he refused to return to the old customs of the Friends. The elders then said that if they persisted, their names would be deleted from the mission's membership book. To this Jacob replied, "Then take them out. Our names are written in the book in heaven."[26]

Ane Marie Rasmussen notes that the Holy Spirit movement started during a period of radical social change and that this movement was a response to the forces of colonialism.[27] In essence, the Holy Spirit movement represented a withdrawal from colonial society, as well as from its missionary sponsors, precisely because the Africans identified missionary Christianity with the conquest of their land. The psychological insecurity and cultural confusion brought on by colonialism resulted in this withdrawal. Interestingly, the withdrawal from society is related to spirit possession because "both are attempts to cope with social tensions."[28] The inability to resist successfully the military, political, and cultural power of Western imperialism compelled the Holy

Spirit people to attribute a distinctive kind of power to the Holy Spirit. "When the Spirit comes to members of the Holy Spirit Churches, what they experience is its strength and power—words used again and again in prayers and sermons. The Holy Spirit can be called 'Lord of Power'"[29] This power is personal in nature, even though its effects may be social. In many Western understandings of spirituality, the spirit is set over and against any structure and hierarchy within the community. In this view spiritual power calls into question the boundaries between groups within the community. Within the African Holy Spirit churches the function of the Holy Spirit is not hindered by the existence of social structure and hierarchy. This is especially evident in the way that persons are empowered for leadership within the Holy Spirit churches:

> [An] important aspect of the Holy Spirit church services is that nearly everybody is a leader of some kind. The organizational levels of village meetings, monthly meetings, quarterly meetings and yearly meetings provide many leadership opportunities. . . . Considering the relatively small number of members in each village congregation, nearly everyone holds one or another of these leadership positions. The amount of influence each individual can exercise in running the church and its services stands in sharp contrast to the opportunities available to exercise influence in the secular society. . . . [The] feeling of fellowship between members is strengthened by nearly everybody being a leader and playing his or her part in running the meetings. In ordinary life these people often have to be passive onlookers to events that threaten their relations with other people. But in the meetings for worship in the Holy Spirit churches a fellowship is created within which each person is important as an active participator, and within which all are free to express themselves. Because of this important function of church services many members want to attend as often as possible, and this is probably why there are so many meetings.[30]

The function of the Holy Spirit in this context is to support a democratic and occasional view of leadership. Leadership is not an ontological trait but a functional role. This view of leadership is quite different from description of African and African American leaders as "charismatic." Despite the often apparently autocratic manner of some African and African American leaders, it should not be forgotten that this authority is ultimately granted by the followers. The same spirit that gives rise to one leader can, and often does, give rise to others.

The story of the Holy Spirit churches is an account of an accommodation of African spirituality to new and strange circumstances. While the members of these churches did not see themselves as social activists, their refusal to ignore the movement of the spirit in their midst was itself considered a social protest.

The institutionalization of African spirituality in the United States provides an instructive complement to the story of the Holy Spirit churches in East Africa. The Black Spiritual churches in the United States emerged during the first two decades of the twentieth century. They took root in larger cities, primarily Chicago, along with more traditional forms of African American Protestantism.[31] It was in the South, however, particularly the city of New Orleans, where the Black Spiritual churches flowered:

> If indeed the Black Spiritual movement started in Chicago, its development in New Orleans appears to have been of vital importance in determining its present content. Although there was much opposition in the South to American Spiritualism, which began in 1848 in upstate New York with the mysterious rappings from the spirit world that the Fox sisters claimed to have heard in their home, it nevertheless spread to cities such as Memphis, Macon, Charleston, and New Orleans. . . . Perhaps in part because its doctrines were favorable to equality and liberalism, as well as compatible with African religions, Spiritualism found adherents among the Black population of the South.[32]

African spirituality as embodied in the Black Spiritual churches lent a dimension of protest to black religion. What distinguishes these churches from black Protestant churches is "their emphasis on the manipulation of one's present condition through magico-religious rituals and esoteric knowledge."[33] It is not coincidental that these churches emerged just as a major social transformation from an agricultural society to an industrial society was occurring in the United States. This transformation also involved mass immigration from various parts of Europe to the United States, as well as a mass migration of African Americans from the South to the North. Hans A. Baer notes that "the Black Spiritual movement, like other new sectarian developments in the Black community, took place within the context of a changing American political economy that forced increasing numbers of Blacks from the rural South to seek employment in urban areas. It was one of many ways that churchgoing Blacks responded to the racist and stratified structure of capitalist America."[34]

Like the Holy Spirit churches of East Africa, the African American spiritual churches provided opportunities for empowerment to women that were not generally available in the wider society. In these churches women often compensated for their relative powerlessness in the secular world by participating and even sometimes rising to positions of leadership in these religious movements.[35] In fact, these churches often provided opportunities for women to have their ministries recognized in ways that they would not be recognized in other African American Protestant communities. These spiritual churches, also like the Holy Spirit churches in East Africa, provided a supportive and cohesive community for their members that was not easily found in other sectors of their lives.

Spiritual churches are sometimes thought of as "otherworldly" or "ascetic." In actuality, "spiritual religion concerns itself with the concrete problems and needs of its adherents and clients."[36] It is not simply this practical focus of African American spiritual religion which is distinctive, however. The methods and strategies employed to ameliorate those social problems involve the "magico-religious" manipulation of one's circumstances. The methods are generally derived from the use of "medicines" in traditional African spirituality and are often seen as in tension with strategies used in mainline Christian communities to effect social transformation. In traditional Western Christian thought the manipulation of the visible social and political order is viewed as the way to change one's life circumstances. This manipulation is possible, however, only if one has access to the channels of power and influence within society. Among persons who are poor, marginalized, and disenfranchised, however, one way to change life's circumstances that does not require access to social and political influence is the manipulation of the invisible spiritual order. Both the manipulation of the visible social and political order and the manipulation of the invisible spiritual order are avenues to social transformation. They both seek to alter the conditions of life and to make it more humane. The two different methods are nonetheless based on two different understandings of the nature of society and social transformation. The former sees society as an organization; and the transformation of that society is best concieved as *correction, adjustment, or even tearing down and rebuilding.* The latter model sees society as more of a living organism, and the transformation of that society is best concieved as *healing, purging, or even death and resurrection.* Both of these perspectives address the issue of social transformation, but within the context of late modernism the organizational model is normally more easily embraced.

The spiritual churches in Africa and the United States meet the deep-seated needs of their members. They provide opportunities for leadership, and they provide a sense of community that undergirds the self-esteem of the members. Still, the spiritual churches tend to play a compensatory role in that they often substitute spiritual status for social status.[37] This tendency points to the power and attractiveness of spiritual churches in the lives of individual members, but the full power of the spiritual churches will not be realized until the personal transformation of individual lives becomes more clearly the public transformation of the social order.

This personal transformational aspect of the spiritual churches has taken on an additional distinctive (and ironic) cast in the United States. Hans Baer argues that these churches encourage their members to embrace the mainstream American values of individualism and materialism.[38] In spite of the outward emphasis on the creation and maintenance of community, these churches often preach a gospel of individualism:

> The advice that Spiritual leaders impart to their followers and clients tends to focus on individualistic concerns. Life in modern America, particularly in large urban areas, is characterized by increasing privatization, or . . . "individuation.". . . Instead of pointing out how social and economic forces may be at the root of many of their followers' and clients' problems, this approach holds the individual responsible for his or her own failures.[39]

In spite of the outward emphasis on the primacy of the spiritual order, these churches often measure the efficacy of their gospel by the materialistic acquisitions of their members. These churches "tend to emphasize the acquisition of 'the good life' along with its worldly pleasures."[40] Theologically, this emphasis on material goods can be defended as the outward and visible sign of and inward and invisible blessing. Yet the question is: At what point does the outward, material sign obscure the inward, spiritual blessing? The fact that these churches, which preach the primacy of community and spirit, also emphasize the twin modernist values of individualism and materialism is a poignant irony. This is perhaps the reason that the full potential of these churches to contribute substantively to the social transformation of society has yet to be realized. We began this chapter by asking: How can we reconceptualize the relationship between spiritual renewal and social transformation so that we might be whole again? While it is not possible to address this question fully in the context of this chapter, we will conclude by suggesting an outline of a spirituality that might address our need for both personal conversion and social transformation.

We Shall All Be Changed: A Spirituality for New Life

When communities are fractured, a spirituality for new life is needed. This spirituality should recognize that authentic liberation from the forces of sin and death requires both personal spiritual renewal and public social transformation.[41] At least three features should mark this spirituality. First, this spirituality will recognize that personal renewal and social transformation involve real human work. The concept of human work and its relation to the divine economy has evolved and developed in complex ways in the Western Christian tradition. For our purposes, however, the notion of human work and its relation to the social order can be described in two distinctive ways in that tradition. In the first way, human work is seen as ultimately insignificant in the future of the social order because the world will end in annihilation (*annihilatio mundi*):

> If the world will be annihilated and a new one created *ex nihilo*, then mundane work has only earthly significance for the well-being of the worker, the worker's community, and posterity—until the day when "the heavens will pass away with a loud noise, and the elements will be dissolved with fire" (2 Pet. 3:10). Since the results of the cumulative work of humankind throughout history will become naught in the final apocalyptic catastrophe, human work is devoid of direct ultimate significance.[42]

The belief that the world will end in catastrophic destruction does not mean that there is no place for human work in the order of things. It does mean, however, that human work has no constituitive role in the redemption of the social order because the fate of the world is sealed due to its sinful nature. In this view the goal of work is to supply the needs of the individual, to provide a disciplined means of pursuing certain ambitions, and the like; but human work itself has no theological significance. In the second way of viewing the relation between human work and the world order, human work is the means by which the world itself is transformed (*transformatio mundi*):

> The picture changes radically with the assumption that the world will end not in apocalyptic destruction but in eschatological transformation. Then the results of the cumulative work of human beings have intrinsic value and gain ultimate significance, for they are related to the eschatological new creation, not only indirectly through the faith and service they enable or sanctification they further, but also directly: the noble

104

products of human ingenuity . . . will be cleansed from impurity, perfect-ed, and transfigured to become a part of God's new creation.[43]

A spirituality for new life requires a positive view of the role of human work in transforming the social order. Work can neither be denigrated nor romanticized. It should be seen as purposeful human activity directed toward the goal of the redemption of the created order.

A second feature of a spirituality for new life is the affirmation that the work of renewal and transformation is inseparable from the quest for survival, liberation, and wholeness. This relationship is clearly seen in the development of womanist spirituality. Black women's spirituality, as an expression of the spirituality of black people in general, is the sum of those actions, beliefs, and rituals that attest to the unmistakable pres-ence of God in daily life:

> The spiritual lives of Black People in the United States have historically extended beyond church, beyond mosque and temple, spilling over into mundane aspects of living and into daily existence. Transcending institu-tional expression, African-African spirituality has flourished outside of sectarian boundaries, permeating the private sphere and the public realm, filling the spaces where everyday needs are considered and met.[44]

The work of survival, liberation and wholeness is, in part, an inner struggle. This struggle is may be aptly characterized as a *spiritual wrestling*:

> Wrestling is a profound metaphor for spiritual struggle, then, because it suggests three aspects of spiritual transformation. . . . It suggests, first, that spiritual growth and change normally come about as a result of confronting opponents, whether external or internal or both. . . . Sec-ondly, it suggests that such encounters, filled though they may be with rage, hatred, and even murderous violence, are also an expression of love, that is, of the desire for relatedness and reunion with the "other." . . . Thirdly, the courage to fight, and the self transformation which can occur in spiritual wrestling, will most likely be experienced as a gift from beyond the self. . . .[45]

This image of wrestling with both internal and external adversaries points to the personal dimension of spiritual work and expresses the profound challenge of finding the proper relationship between the need for self-preservation, the desire for freedom, and the hope for reunion with other souls.

Womanist spirituality is also a struggle within the public spaces in which African American women and others live. As such, this spirituality is connected to the efforts of black women to ameliorate concrete social problems. In the nineteenth century in the United States black women's spirituality found public expression in many of the moral reform societies of the day. These societies were devoted to the elimination of prostitution, alcohol consumption, and other practices deemed detrimental to the family. This focus on the family was, in many instances, the only acceptable way for black women to effect a more general social transformation. Emilie M. Townes observes that "the focus of moral reform societies was on the family as an arena to solve larger social problems."[46] Marcia Y. Riggs also notes that within black women's experience "social problems were perceived as moral problems, and voluntary social reform efforts (e.g., temperance unions, mission societies, aid associations, women's clubs) were designed to eliminate corruption."[47] While black women participated with white women in many of these moral reform movements, the motivation of black women was clearly rooted in the empowerment granted by the spirit of God:

> African American women began with an intense personal experience of the divine in their lives and took that call to salvation into the public realm to reform a corrupt moral order. Their spirituality, which at first viewing resembles a self-centered piety with little relation to the larger context, is an excellent example of the linking of personal and social transformation to effect salvation and thereby bring in the new heaven and new earth. These women sought perfection and advocated social reform in the framework of a spirituality that valued life and took seriously the responsibility to help create and maintain a just and moral social order.[48]

The spirituality of black women could not be contained within the images of domesticity regnant in the nineteenth and early twentieth centuries. The transformative work of black women was about family, but the family was more than a basic economic unit, a racial clan, or a geographical tribe. The family, in the view of these black women, was a name for community. Black women's spirituality that focused on the redemption and empowerment of the family was by definition a social spirituality. Emilie Townes reminds us that "a womanist spirituality is concrete, particular, universal, relevant, relentless, self-critical, communal. In short, it is social witness. . . ."[49]

The third feature of a spirituality for new life is the Holy Spirit as its source. One of the most forgotten topics in contemporary discussions on spirituality is the role of the Holy Spirit. A spirituality for new life is based on the affirmation that renewal and transformation are the work of the Holy Spirit in the world. The Holy Spirit is the ongoing presence of God in Christ with us. It is the gift of the resurrection of Jesus, which both renews and transforms. The resurrection proclaims the renewal of the created order, calling it back to primal faithfulness to and relationship with God. The Holy Spirit is that power which continually renews life, animates human history, and validates the cosmos, confirming the beauty and aptness of God's initial design. The resurrection proclaims the transformation of the created order, calling it forward to a new hope and life in God. The Holy Spirit is that power which continually transforms life, directs human history, and guides the cosmos, confirming the passion and care of God. The work of the Holy Spirit in the world calls humanity to task because it is on the continuum between renewal and transformation that moral discernment and ethical reflection take place. It is in the tension between excavating the past and building the future, between conservation and innovation, that spiritual work is required.

Understanding the work of the Holy Spirit is important in this context because it provides the structural model or paradigm for human spiritual work in the world. In his fine work, *Winds of the Spirit*, Peter C. Hodgson identifies the work of the Spirit as having two dimensions: the liberation of the world and the perfection of God.[50] The first work of the Holy Spirit is to mediate the presence of God to the world in such a way that God's will is done on earth. "The expression 'liberation of the world' gathers up the whole process of the return of the world from alienated otherness and separateness to its end in divine life."[51] The second work of the Holy Spirit is to call the created order into the divine life so that the freedom of God is perfected in heaven as it is on earth. "The expression 'perfection of God' or 'freedom of God' identifies the goal of this process in terms of what it means for the divine life itself (the triune figuration of God) and for the consummation of the world in God, its sanctification. The first work of the Spirit is cosmological and historical, while the second work is eschatological and historical."[52] A spirituality for new life is concerned with affirmation and validation in both the human community and within the community of the divine life. A spirituality for new life is concerned with leadership and guidance in both the human quest for fulfillment and the quest for fulfillment in the life of God. Social problems are occasions for reflection and action directed toward the transformation of the social order. Theological problems are occasions for reflection and action directed toward the renewal of our spiritual lives. Every single genuine prayer is an acknowledgment that we need change in our lives. This change cannot be reduced to self-improvement, although that is important. Nor can it be reduced to the design and implementation of new social policies, although that, too, is important. The fact is that both the body politic and individual bodies have been and continue to be hurt by inhumane actions and attitudes. Shame, disease, and hopelessness are three of the names of our griefs. We need "to make the wounded whole." While the pain and suffering of humankind provide the occasion for a spirituality for new life, the joy that animates it is captured in the resurrection proclamation of the Apostle Paul to the church at Corinth, "We shall all be changed!"

Notes

1. Social Problems as Theological Problems

1. See James H. Evans, Jr., "Toward An Afro-American Theology," *Journal of Religious Thought* 40 (Fall/Winter 1984): 39–54; and *We Have Been Believers: An African-American Systematic Theology* (Minneapolis: Fortress Press, 1992), 3–9.

2. John Macquarrie, *Principles of Christian Theology*, 2d ed. (New York: Scribner's, 1977), 40.

3. David Tracy, *The Analogical Imagination: Christian Theology and the Culture of Pluralism* (New York: Crossroad, 1981), 6ff.

4. Friedrich Schleiermacher, *Brief Outline on the Study of Theology*, William Farrer, trans. (Edinburgh: T&T Clark, 1850), 91–94.

5. Gerhard Ebeling, *The Study of Theology* (Philadelphia: Fortress Press, 1978), 118.

6. Hugo Assmann, *Theology for a Nomad Church* (Maryknoll, N.Y.: Orbis Books), 29.

7. William M. Sullivan, "The Public Intellectual as Transgressor? Addressing the Disconnection between Expert and Civil Culture" in *Higher Education Exchange*, (Dayton, Ohio: The Kettering Foundation, 1996), 18.

8. Don S. Browning, *A Fundamental Practical Theology: Descriptive and Strategic Proposals* (Minneapolis: Fortress Press, 1991), 36.

9. William E. Cole and Charles H. Miller, *Social Problems: A Sociological Interpretation* (New York: David McKay Co., 1965), 6.

10. Henry George, *Social Problems* (New York: Doubleday, 1911), 1–2.

11. Raymond W. Murray and Frank T. Flynn, *Social Problems* (New York: F. S. Crofts, 1938), 5.

12. F. James Davis, *Social Problems: Enduring Major Issues and Social Change* (New York: The Free Press, 1970), 21–22.

13. Howard S. Becker, ed., *Social Problems: A Modern Approach* (New York: John Wiley & Sons, 1966), 2.

14. Cole and Miller, *Social Problems*, 4.

15. Malcolm Spector and John I. Kitsuse, *Constructing Social Problems* (Menlo Park, Calif.: Cummings Pub. Co., 1977), 73–76. This highly original and perceptive perspective on the nature of social problems has given rise to a significant body of responding literature. Cf. Joel Best, ed. *Images of Issues: Typifying Contemporary Social Problems* (New York: Aldine De Gruyter, 1989). In addition, important clar-

Notes

ifications and modifications of this view have also emerged. Cf. Peter R. Ibarra and John I. Kitsuse, "Vernacular Constituents of Moral Discourse: An Interactionist Proposal for the Study of Social Problems," in Gale Miller and James A. Holstein, eds., *Constructivist Controversies: Issues in Social Problems Theory* (New York: Aldine De Gruyter, 1993), 21–54.

16. Spector and Kitsuse, *Constructing Social Problems,* 78, 79, 83.

17. Ibid., 86–87.

18. Ibid., 84.

19. Gordon D. Kaufman, *God the Problem* (Cambridge, Mass.: Harvard University Press, 1972), 7.

20. Gordon D. Kaufman, *In Face of Mystery: A Constructive Theology* (Cambridge, Mass.: Harvard University Press, 1993), 60–61.

21. Ibid., 233.

22. Ibid., 238.

23. George A. Lindbeck, *The Nature of Doctrine: Religion and Theology in a Postliberal Age* (Philadelphia: Westminster Press, 1984).

24. Ibid., 16.

25. Ibid., 32–33.

26. Ibid., 35, 82, 84.

27. Ibid., 35.

28. Ibid., 40–41.

29. W. E. B. Du Bois, *The Souls of Black Folk* (New York: Penguin Books, 1995 [1903]), 54.

30. Examples are *The Negro Problem: A Series of Articles by Representative American Negroes of To-day* (New York: James Pott & Co., 1903); and Julia E. Johnsen, comp., *The Negro Problem* (New York: H. W. Wilson Co., 1921). A more virulent debate occurred in 1849 in England between Thomas Carlyle and John Stuart Mill. This debate was spurred by the publication of a treatise by Carlyle to which he intentionally gave the offensive title, "The Nigger Question." See Eugene R. August, ed., *Thomas Carlyle, The Nigger Question; John Stuart Mill, The Negro Question* (New York: Meredith Corp., 1971).

31. C. Wright Mills, *The Sociological Imagination* (New York: Oxford University Press, 1959), 8.

32. Du Bois, *The Souls of Black Folk,* 43–44.

33. Ibid., 45.

34. Fannie Barrier Williams, "The Colored Girl," in Mary Helen Washington, ed., *Invented Lives: Narratives of Black Women 1860–1960* (New York: Doubleday Books, 1987), 150.

35. Du Bois, *The Souls of Black Folk,* 45.

36. Toni Morrison, "Unspeakable Things Unspoken: The Afro-American Presence in American Literature," in Angelyn Mitchell, ed., *Within the Circle: An Anthology of African American Literary Criticism from the Harlem Renaissance to the Present* (Durham, N.C.: Duke University Press, 1994), 377.

2. Honor, Shame, and Grace

1. Richard J. Herrnstein and Charles Murray, *The Bell Curve: Intelligence and Class Structure in American Life* (New York: The Free Press, 1994), 470, 473.

2. Shelby Steele, *The Content of Our Character: A New Vision of Race in America* (New York: HarperCollins, 1991).

3. Cornel West, "Unmasking the Black Conservative," *The Christian Century* (July 16, 1986), 644–47.

4. *Honour and Shame: The Values of Mediterranean Society*, ed. J. G. Peristiany (Chicago: University of Chicago Press, 1966), 9. In the Introduction to this standard-bearer collection of essays in the field, the editor notes that "Mediterranean honour and shame were first discussed by the present group of authors in 1959 at Burg Wartenstein, the European Headquarters of the Wenner-Gren Foundation."

5. Julio Caro Baroja, "Honour and Shame: A Historical Account of Several Conflicts," in Peristiany, *Honour and Shame*, 81.

6. A particularly helpful resource in this area is Charles Taylor's essay, "The Politics of Recognition," in Amy Gutman, ed., *Multiculturalism and "The Politics of Recognition"* (Princeton, N.J.: Princeton University Press, 1992), 25–74.

7. Julian Pitt-Rivers, "Honor," in *The International Encyclopedia of the Social Sciences*, David L. Sills, ed., vol. 6 (New York: Macmillan, 1968), 503–04.

8. Julian Pitt-Rivers, "Honour and Social Status," in Peristiany, *Honour and Shame*, 22.

9. Nicholas Fotion and Gerard Elfstrom, "Honor," in Lawrence C. Becker, ed., *Encyclopedia of Ethics*, vol. 1 (New York: Garland Publishing, 1992), 555.

10. Pitt-Rivers, "Honor," 507.

11. Fotion and Elfstrom, "Honor," 555.

12. Pitt-Rivers, "Honor," 509.

13. See Anton Blok, "Rams and Billy Goats: A Key to the Mediterranean Code of Honour," in Eric R. Wolf, ed., *Religion, Power and Protest in Local Communities* (New York: Mouton Publishers, 1984), 51–70.

14. Pitt-Rivers, "Honour and Social Status," in Peristiany, *Honour and Shame*, 29.

15. Pitt-Rivers, "Honor," 506.

16. Pitt-Rivers, "Honour and Social Status," 70.

17. John Rawls, *A Theory of Justice* (Cambridge, Mass.: Harvard University Press, 1971), 442.

18. Ibid., 446.

19. *Shame and Its Sisters: A Silvan Tomkins Reader*, ed. Eve Kosofsky Sedwick and Adam Frank (Durham, N.C.: Duke University Press, 1995), 133. "The private parts are the seat of shame, vulnerable to the public view and represented symbolically in the gestures and verbal expressions of desecration" (Julian Pitt-Rivers, "Honor," 505).

20. Tomkins, *Shame and Its Sisters*, 136. "The loss of honor is equated with the loss of life, 'for according to the Sages who made the ancient laws, two crimes are equal, to kill a man or to accuse him of wrong-doing; for a man once he is defamed, although he be innocent, is dead to the good and to the honour of the world'" (Julio Caro Baroja, "Honour and Shame," 85).

21. *Shame and Its Sisters*, 139.

22. Julio Caro Baroja, "Honour and Shame," 101.

23. Lila Abu-Lughod, "Honor and the Sentiments of Loss in a Bedouin Society," *American Ethnologist* 12/2 (May, 1985): 257.

24. Pitt-Rivers, "Honor," 510.

25. Orlando Patterson, *Slavery and Social Death: A Comparative Study* (Cambridge, Mass.: Harvard University Press, 1982), 84–96.

Notes

26. Ibid., 78.

27. See Toni Morrison, *Beloved* (New York: Alfred A. Knopf, 1987), 107ff.

28. Evelyn Brooks Higginbotham, *Righteous Discontent: The Women's Movement in the Black Baptist Church, 1880–1920* (Cambridge, Mass.: Harvard University Press, 1993), 185–229.

29. From Ms. Franklin's recorded song, "Respect," by Otis Redding (East Memphis–Time–Redwal, BMI). Originally released April 10, 1967 on Atlantic Records 2403.

30. Although the focus of this section is the New Testament, a discussion of the function of honor and shame in the Hebrew Bible can be found in Saul M. Olyan's essay "Honor, Shame, and Covenant Relations in Ancient Israel and Its Environment," in *Journal of Biblical Literature* 115/2 (Summer 1996): 201–18.

31. Bruce J. Malina and Jerome H. Neyrey, "Honor and Shame in Luke-Acts: Pivotal Values of the Mediterranean World," in Jerome H. Neyrey, ed., *The Social World of Luke-Acts: Models for Interpretation* (Peabody, Mass.: Hendrickson Publishers, 1991), 25–65.

32. Ibid., 42.

33. Ibid., 41–42.

34. Ibid., 32.

35. Ibid., 33.

36. Ibid., 28–29. Luke certainly emphasizes Jesus' honor as ascribed by virtue of divine birth. Yet there is the subordinant theme of honor by acquisition. This raises interesting christological questions. Does ascribed honor support traditional incarnational Christologies? Does acquired honor support adoptionist Christologies?

37. Booker T. Washington, *Up from Slavery* (New York: Oxford University Press, 1995).

38. Halvor Moxnes, "Honor and Shame," *Biblical Theology Bulletin* 23/4 (Winter 1993): 167–76.

39. See Halvor Moxnes, "Honor and Righteousness in Romans," *Journal for the Study of the New Testament* 32 (1988): 61–77; cf. Halvor Moxnes, "Honor, Shame, and the Outside World in Paul's Letter to the Romans," in *The Social World of Formative Christianity and Judaism*, ed. Jacob Neusner et al. (Philadelphia: Fortress Press, 1988), 207–18.

40. Moxnes, "Honor and Righteousness in Romans," 64–65.

41. Ibid., 66.

42. Ibid.

43. Ibid., 67.

44. Ibid., 74.

45. Ibid., 73.

46. Arthur J. Dewey, "A Matter of Honor: A Social-Historical Analysis of 2 Corinthians 10," *Harvard Theological Review* 78/1–2 (January/April, 1985): 209–17.

47. Moxnes, "Honour and Righteousness in Romans," 69.

48. Dewey, "A Matter of Honor: A Social-Historical Analysis of 2 Corinthians 10," 216.

49. J. G. Peristiany and Julian Pitt-Rivers, eds., *Honor and Grace in Anthropology* (New York: Cambridge University Press, 1992).

50. Julian Pitt-Rivers, "Postscript: The Place of Grace in Anthropology," in *Honor and Grace in Anthropology*, 215.

51. Ibid., 231.

52. Dottie Rambo, "He Looked Beyond My Fault" (Nashville: HeartWarming Music Co., 1968). Used by permission.

3. Health, Disease, and Salvation

1. See William F. May, "The Ethical Foundations of Health Care Reform," *The Christian Century* (June 1–8, 1994), 573; and Allen D. Verhey, "The Health Security Act: Policy and Story," *The Christian Century* (January 26, 1994), 74.

2. "The Ethics of Health Care: An Interview with C. Everett Koop," *The Christian Century* (January 26, 1994), 78.

3. Verhey, "The Health Security Act," 76.

4. "Health Reform and Civic Survival: An Interview with Quentin D. Young," *The Christian Century* (November 2, 1994), 1014.

5. Toni Morrison, *Playing in the Dark: Whiteness and the Literary Imagination* (Cambridge, Mass.: Harvard University Press, 1992).

6. See Frederick F. Cartwright, *Disease and History* (New York: Dorset Press, 1972).

7. Henry E. Sigerist, *A History of Medicine*, vol. 1 (New York: Oxford University Press, 1951), 38.

8. J. B. deC. M. Saunders, *The Transitions from Ancient Egyptian to Greek Medicine* (Lawrence: University of Kansas Press, 1963), 21.

9. Many of the ideas which made their way into that body of works called the "Hippocratic Collection" bore striking similarity to medical ideas from ancient Egypt.

10. Henry E. Sigerist, *A History of Medicine*, vol. 2 (New York: Oxford University Press, 1961), 20–21.

11. Ibid., 97.

12. Albert S. Lyons and R. Joseph Petrucelli II, *Medicine: An Illustrated History* (New York: Abradale Press, 1978), 207.

13. Ibid., 215.

14. Ibid., 183.

15. Walther Riese, *The Conception of Disease: Its History, Its Versions and Its Nature* (New York: Philosophical Library, 1953), 11.

16. Ibid., 72.

17. Ibid., 62.

18. H. Tristam Englehardt Jr., "Understanding Faith Traditions in the Context of Health Care: Philosophy as a Guide for the Perplexed," in Martin E. Marty and Kenneth L. Vaux, eds., *Health/Medicine and the Faith Traditions: An Inquiry into Religion and Medicine* (Philadelphia: Fortress Press, 1982), 174–75.

19. H. Tristram Engelhardt Jr., "The Social Meanings of Illness," *Second Opinion* 1 (1986): 27.

20. Benjamin Ward Richardson, *Diseases of Modern Life* (New York: Bermingham & Co., 1882).

21. See Barbara Bair and Susan E. Cayleff, ed., *Wings of Gauze: Women of Color and the Experience of Health and Illness* (Detroit: Wayne State University Press, 1993).

22. Sander L. Gilman, *Difference and Pathology: Stereotypes of Sexuality, Race, and Madness* (Ithaca, N.Y.: Cornell University Press, 1985), 101.

Notes

23. Ronald Takaki, *Iron Cages: Race and Culture in Nineteenth-Century America* (New York: Oxford University Press, 1990), 16–17.

24. Ibid., 31.

25. Gilman, *Difference and Pathology*, 137.

26. Ibid., 138.

27. Lyons and Petrucelli, *Medicine: An Illustrated History*, 291.

28. Theophus H. Smith, *Conjuring Culture: Biblical Formations of Black America* (New York: Oxford University Press, 1994), 81–109.

29. Lyons and Petrucelli, *Medicine: An Illustrated History*, 71.

30. Cited in John J. Pilch, "Reading Matthew Anthropologically: Healing in Cultural Perspective," *Listening* 24/3 (Fall 1989): 285.

31. Karen S. Carter, "A Biblical Vision of Wholeness," *Brethren Life and Thought* 33/1 (Winter 1988): 60.

32. Robert M. Price, "Illness Theodicies in the New Testament," *Journal of Religion and Health* 25/4 (Winter 1986): 309–15.

33. See Allan Young, "The Anthropologies of Illness and Sickness," *Annual Review of Anthropology* 11 (1982): 264.

34. John J. Pilch argues that the concept of disease was foreign to the world of Luke-Acts, and that illness is a more appropriate category to juxtapose to health and wholeness. "Sickness and Healing in Luke-Acts," in Jerome H. Neyrey, ed., *The Social World of Luke-Acts: Models for Interpretation* (Peabody, Mass.: Hendrickson Publishers, 1991), 191.

35. Andrew Olu Igenoza, "Medicine and Healing in African Christianity: A Biblical Critique," *African Episcopal Review* 30/1 (February 1988): 15. It is interesting to note how often this notion of health as harmony appears in the medical lore of people outside of the Greco-Roman world. It suggests that the idea has its roots deep within human consciousness.

36. Harvey Cox, "Healers and Ecologists: Pentecostalism in Africa," *The Christian Century* (November 9, 1994), 1044.

37. Peter Worsley, "Non-Western Medical Systems," *Annual Review of Anthropology* 11 (1982): 325.

38. See James N. Lapsley, *Salvation and Health: The Interlocking Processes of Life* (Philadelphia: Westminster Press, 1972), 31–45; and Donald G. Bloesch, *The Christian Life and Salvation* (Grand Rapids, Mich.: Wm. B. Eerdmans, 1967), 33–46.

39. James P. Wind, "Health," in Donald W. Musser and Joseph L. Price, eds., *A New Handbook of Christian Theology* (Abingdon Press: Nashville, 1992), 214.

40. Andrew Sung Park, *The Wounded Heart of God: The Asian Concept of Han and the Christian Doctrine of Sin* (Nashville: Abingdon Press, 1993), 102–3.

41. Worsley, "Non-Western Medical Systems," 322.

42. Cited in Andrew Olu Igenoza, "Medicine and Healing," 23.

4. Hope, Racism, and Community

1. I am indebted to Ms. Kimberly Parsons Chastain of Princeton Theological Seminary for this insight into the derivation of the concept of beloved community.

2. See Marjorie Hewitt Suchocki, *The End of Evil: Process Eschatology in Historical Context* (Albany: State University of New York Press, 1988).

3. See Jürgen Moltmann, *Theology of Hope: On the Ground and the Implications of a Christian Eschatology* (Minneapolis: Fortress Press, 1993 [1967]).

4. See Gustavo Gutiérrez, *A Theology of Liberation: History, Politics, and Salvation* (Maryknoll, N.Y.: Orbis Books, 1967).

5. Rosemary Radford Ruether, *Sexism and Godtalk: Toward a Feminist Theology* (Boston: Beacon Press, 1983), 254.

6. See Gayraud S. Wilmore, *Last Things First* (Philadelphia: Westminster Press, 1982).

7. George M. Frederickson, *White Supremacy: A Comparative Study in American and South African History* (New York: Oxford University Press, 1981), 153.

8. John W. Cell, *The Highest Stage of White Supremacy: The Origins of Segregation in South Africa and the American South* (New York: Cambridge University Press, 1982), 101–2.

9. James A. Aho, *The Politics of Righteousness: Idaho Christian Patriotism* (Seattle: University of Washington Press, 1990), 39, 59.

10. James Ridgeway, *Blood in the Face: The Ku Klux Klan, Aryan Nations, Nazi Skinheads, and the Rise of a New White Culture* (New York: Thunder's Mouth Press, 1990), 79.

11. Aho, *The Politics of Righteousness*, 3.

12. For a journalistic, narrative account of recent activities of white supremacist groups in the United States, see Kevin Flynn and Gary Gerhardt, *The Silent Brotherhood: Inside America's Racist Underground* (New York: The Free Press, 1989).

13. Ridgeway, *Blood in the Face*, 33.

14. Ibid., 34. Although the Klan appealed to populist values, it is interesting to note the development of an ideology of gender equality in the Klan movement in the 1920s. See Kathleen M. Blee, "Gender Ideology and the Role of Women in the 1920s Klan Movement," *Sociological Spectrum* 7 (1987): 73–97.

15. Ridgeway, *Blood in the Face*, 20.

16. Aho, *The Politics of Righteousness*, 59.

17. For an insightful account of the rise of the White Aryan Resistance, see Leonard Zeskind's "Peddling Racist Violence for a New Generation: A Profile of Tom Metzger and the White Aryan Resistance," *Center of Democratic Renewal* (December 1987).

18. Ridgeway, *Blood in the Face*, 111.

19. Ibid., 112.

20. Ibid., 109–41.

21. George D. Kelsey, *Racism and the Christian Understanding of Man* (New York: Charles Scribner's Sons, 1965), 42.

22. Ridgeway, *Blood in the Face*, 17.

23. Ibid., 32.

24. As a young boy growing up in Detroit, I, like all African Americans, was aware that the town of Dearborn, a suburb of Detroit, was all-white, determined to stay that way, and thus was not a safe place for any person of color to be found after dark. It is a curious bit of irony that after years of political maneuvering to keep black people and Jews out of their town, the residents of Dearborn now reside with the newest target of racial hate in the United States, people of Arab descent. Dearborn has the largest Arab population of any city in the United States.

25. Ridgeway, *Blood in the Face*, 40–41.

26. Aho, *The Politics of Righteousness*, 19.

Notes

27. Ibid., 52.
28. Flynn and Gerhardt, *The Silent Brotherhood*, 51.
29. Ridgeway, *Blood in the Face*, 53.
30. Ibid., 54.
31. "Three Thousand Years of Biblical Interpretation with Reference to Black Peoples," in *African American Religious Studies: An Interdisciplinary Anthology*, ed. Gayraud S. Wilmore (Durham, N.C.: Duke University Press, 1989), 105–28.
32. For additional insight into this topic see Cain Hope Felder's *Troubling Biblical Waters: Race, Class, and Family* (Maryknoll, N.Y.: Orbis Books, 1989).
33. Flynn and Gerhardt, *The Silent Brotherhood*, 52. Also see Jonathan R. White, "The Road to Armageddon: Religion and Domestic Terrorism," *Quarterly Journal of Ideology* 13/2:11–21; and Charles B. Strozier, "Christian Fundamentalism, Nazism, and the Millennium," *The Psychohistory Review* 18/2 (Winter 1990): 207–17.
34. Ridgeway, *Blood in the Face*, 150.
35. This is one of the major insights of Malcolm X. See *The Autobiography of Malcolm X* (New York: Random House, 1964).
36. Racial purity is not to be confused with racial or cultural integrity. The latter stresses the inherent gifts that reside in a given cultural or ethnic group, while the former is based on a negative evaluation of "the other race," and an implied vulnerability of the race seeking to maintain its purity.
37. Ridgeway, *Blood in the Face*, 169.
38. Kathryn E. Tanner, *The Politics of God: Christian Theologies and Social Justice* (Minneapolis: Fortress Press, 1992), 42.
39. Martin Luther King Jr., "Showdown for Nonviolence," in *A Testament of Hope: The Essential Speeches and Writings of Martin Luther King, Jr.*, ed. James M. Washington (San Francisco: Harper & Row, 1986), 71.
40. Vincent Harding, *Hope and History: Why We Must Share the Story of the Movement* (Maryknoll, N.Y.: Orbis Books, 1990), 190.

5. Spiritual Renewal and Social Transformation

1. See James H. Evans Jr., "African American Christianity and the Postmodern Condition," *Journal of the American Academy of Religion* 58/2 (1990): 207–22.
2. Nestor Jaen, S.J., *Toward a Liberation Spirituality* (Chicago: Loyola University Press, 1991), 12.
3. Peter F. Drucker, "The Age of Social Transformation," *Atlantic Monthly* (November, 1994), 53.
4. Ibid., 54.
5. Ibid.
6. Ibid.
7. Ibid., 56.
8. Ibid., 76.
9. Ibid.
10. Ibid., 66.
11. Ibid., 78.
12. Ibid., 63.
13. Peter J. Paris, *The Spirituality of African Peoples: The Search for a Common Moral Discourse* (Minneapolis: Fortress Press, 1995), 22.

14. Ibid.

15. Robert Farris Thompson, *Flash of the Spirit: African and Afro-American Art and Philosophy* (New York: Random House, 1984), xiii.

16. Ibid., 139.

17. Ibid., 117.

18. Ibid., 118. These notions of spirit-embodying medicines and spirit-directing medicines bear an interesting relation to the classical pneumatological emphases on the preserving and transforming work of the Holy Spirit.

19. Patrick A. Kalilombe, "Spirituality in the African Perspective," in Rosino Gibellini, ed., *Paths of African Theology* (Maryknoll, N.Y.: Orbis Books, 1994), 122.

20. Ibid., 128.

21. Ibid., 117.

22. Ibid., 132. One of the major conflicts between African spirituality and Western Christian spirituality is centered around the meaning of marriage. Cf. Benezet Bujo, *African Theology in Its Social Context* (Maryknoll, N.Y.: Orbis Books, 1992), chap. 13.

23. George Cummings, "The Slave Narratives as a Source of Black Theological Discourse: The Spirit and Eschatology," in Dwight N. Hopkins and George Cummings, eds., *Cut Loose Your Stammering Tongue: Black Theology in the Slave Narratives* (Maryknoll, N.Y.: Orbis Books, 1991), 46–66.

24. One of the major arguments of Gayraud S. Wilmore's classic work, *Black Religion and Black Radicalism* (Maryknoll, N.Y.: Orbis Books, 1983), is that the spirit of radicalism often found more receptive avenues of expression outside the institutional churches.

25. Ane Marie Rasmussen, *Modern African Spirituality: The Independent Holy Spirit Churches in East Africa, 1902–1976* (London: British Academic Press, 1996), 11.

26. Ibid., 18.

27. Ibid., 27.

28. Ibid.

29. Ibid., 123.

30. Ibid., 91–92.

31. Hans A. Baer, *The Black Spiritual Movement: A Religious Response to Racism* (Knoxville: University of Tennessee Press, 1984), 17–18.

32. Ibid, 18.

33. Ibid., 9.

34. Ibid., 17.

35. Ibid., 164.

36. Ibid., 169.

37. Ibid., 163.

38. Ibid., 160.

39. Ibid., 183.

40. Ibid., 179.

41. Robert Michael Franklin, *Liberating Visions: Human Fulfillment and Social Justice in African American Thought* (Minneapolis: Fortress Press, 1990), 2.

42. Miroslav Volf, *Work in the Spirit: Toward a Theology of Work* (New York: Oxford University Press, 1991), 89.

43. Ibid., 91.

Notes

44. Yvonne Patricia Chireau, "Hidden Traditions: Black Religion, Magic and Alternative Spiritual Beliefs in Womanist Perspective," in Jacquelyn Grant, ed., *Perspectives on Womanist Theology* (Atlanta: ITC Press, 1995), 68.

45. William H. Becker, "Celie as Spiritual Wrestler," in Jacquelyn Grant, ed., *Perspectives on Womanist Theology*, 151.

46. Emilie M. Townes, *In a Blaze of Glory: Womanist Spirituality as Social Witness* (Nashville: Abingdon Press, 1995), 35.

47. Marcia Y. Riggs, *Awake, Arise & Act: A Womanist Call for Black Liberation* (Cleveland: Pilgrim Press, 1994), 64.

48. Ibid., 36.

49. Ibid., 121.

50. Peter C. Hodgson, *Winds of the Spirit: A Constructive Christian Theology* (Louisville: Westminster John Knox, 1994).

51. Ibid., 291.

52. Ibid., 292.

Index

Index

Index

Index